LEWIS AND CLARK IN THE ILLINOIS COUNTRY: THE LITTLE-TOLD STORY

Robert E. Hartley

Library of Congress Number: 2002092024
ISBN :   Hardcover   1-4010-5794-2
           Softcover   1-4010-5793-4

Jacket illustration and design by A. J. Hartley.

Lewis and Clark portraits by Charles Willson Peale, courtesy of Independence National Historic Park, Philadelphia.

Map illustration derived from Victor Collot map of 1796, courtesy of Edward E. Ayer Collection, The Newberry Library, Chicago.

Material from *The Field Notes of Captain William Clark, 1803-1805,* William Clark author, Ernest Staples Osgood, editor, reprinted with permission of the Yale University Press, New Haven, CT.

Sniktau Publications
P.O. Box 350368
Westminster, CO 80035-0368

This book was printed in the United States of America.

To order additional copies of this book, contact:
Xlibris Corporation
1-888-795-4274
www.Xlibris.com
Orders@Xlibris.com
15273

To Mary; and for Chris, Taylor and Ian

Other Books by Robert E. Hartley

Charles H. Percy: A Political Perspective

Big Jim Thompson of Illinois

Diamond in the Emerald City: The Story of Safeco Field (editor)

Paul Powell of Illinois: A Lifelong Democrat

CONTENTS

ILLUSTRATIONS

PREFACE

Fragmentary reports of Meriwether Lewis and William Clark's time in the Illinois country have been around for decades. Some are included in the journals of the captains and other members of the expedition during 1803 and 1804. Documents unearthed by historians, notably the letters between Thomas Jefferson and Meriwether Lewis, added to the picture. The field notes of William Clark, discovered in the 1950s and published in 1964, provided fresh details of the winter at Camp Dubois on the Wood River.

Until now, however, there has been little attempt to give the winter Lewis and Clark spent in the Illinois country a comprehensive look. The objective of this narrative is to consider Lewis and Clark, the people they met, and the land on which they lived temporarily, as one story, by bringing the fragments together with additional documentary information. The result is a more complete—although surely not final—picture of what occurred during almost six months from November, 1803, to May, 1804, and why. By exploring in depth the time before the expedition started up the Missouri River the overall account of the historic expedition to the Pacific Coast is enhanced.

Essential to the full view is an understanding of the complex combination of geography and history of the Illinois country. The familiar sites mentioned in existing works tell us where Lewis and Clark spent time along the Mississippi River, with special attention devoted to Camp Dubois, site of the winter camp. However, the extended perspective considers Illinois people and their experiences, as discovered by Lewis and Clark in Kaskaskia, Cahokia, St. Louis and at Camp Dubois on the Wood River. Clarence

Walworth Alvord, one of the first historians to explore the depth and breadth of the Illinois country, provides helpful background in this description from his book *The Illinois Country, 1673-1818:*
"The location of the land as well as its fertility has shaped its destiny. The territory of the state touches the watershed of the Great Lakes on the north, is washed on the west by the Mississippi river, and extends to the Ohio on the south. Resting in the heart of the Mississippi Valley, the Illinois country has been shaken by every great force stirring the continent; the north and the south, the east and the west have exercised formative influences on its destiny . . ."

In the context offered by Alvord, people of the Illinois country drained information from a vast territory beyond the boundaries of the state today, from St. Louis and early Missouri settlements, and the full range of the Ohio and Mississippi River valleys, and placed it before the Corps of Discovery.

Then, drawing on their experiences as frontiersmen and soldiers, the captains merged the raw material from the Illinois country with intelligence gathered by President Thomas Jefferson and his associates. From this, Meriwether Lewis and William Clark prepared themselves for the extraordinary adventure that opened the western United States.

For years, residents living in proximity to the site where Lewis and Clark spent the winter of 1803-04 wanted something more than an obscure signpost to mark the place and its significance. They pleaded for an attraction that would explain to visitors the importance of Camp Dubois to the expedition. Their wishes have been granted. A new chapter in the state's commemoration of the campsite has been written.

The Illinois Historic Preservation Agency, headquartered in Springfield—with cooperation from the National Park Service, and countless interested citizens from southwestern Illinois—has created the Lewis and Clark State Historic Site near Hartford, Illinois, at the approximate location of Camp Dubois, given changes in river channels.

Inside the interpretive center are exhibits that describe what life was like in the Illinois country of that time, and the expectations for the expedition. The centerpiece exhibit portrays in detail the time spent by the Corps at Camp Dubois. The presentation concludes with an analysis of the legacy of Lewis and Clark. When completed the site will include a replica of Camp Dubois.

Visitors to the site now will have an opportunity to understand the Illinois role in the Lewis and Clark saga.

ACKNOWLEDGMENTS

In the summer of 1970 my wife, Mary, and I read the journals of Lewis and Clark as edited by Elliott Coues. The following year our two children joined us on a motor trip that followed the expedition's route from Illinois to the headwaters of the Missouri River, and the Bitterroot Mountains. Our first taste of the Voyage of Discovery made us hungry for more.

Since then the captains' journey has been a constant companion. At the same time a continuing interest in Illinois history led to a curiosity about the time Lewis and Clark spent in the Illinois country, and a discovery that the story is mostly overlooked in literature of the expedition. With the 200th anniversary of the journey at hand, it is time to explore the Illinois saga in greater detail.

When tackling a subject that is so much a part of American history, the debts accumulate rapidly. Among those who have carried the research load in an array of publications on Lewis and Clark are Donald Jackson, Gary Moulton, James Ronda, and Ernest S. Osgood. An understanding of the Mississippi River valley and territorial Illinois came from the works of Abraham Nasatir, Clarence Walworth Alvord, Theodore Pease, John Francis McDermott, and James E. Davis.

Research compiled by Peggy Turk Sinko and Delores Swekel helped open doors to the lives of Illinoisans. I benefited from the extensive resources available at the Newberry Library, the Chicago Historical Society, the Detroit Public Library, and the Denver Public Library.

E. Cheryl Schnirring at the Illinois State Library handled requests with patience and thoroughness. Mary Michals once again dug into the library's vast photographic resources for Illinois illustrations. Bill Whiteside, no kin to the Whiteside family of early Illinois, generously shared his impressive genealogical file about the family.

Stephen Kerber and Amanda Bahr Evola, who manage archives and collections at the Lovejoy Library at Southern Illinois University-Edwardsville, led me through the papers of John Francis McDermott. The fine staff of the Missouri Historical Society assisted in locating documents on events and people connected to Lewis and Clark. Staff at the Belleville, Illinois, public library counseled on matters of St. Clair County history. D. G. Schumacher, Paul Simon, Carolyn Hennessy, David Kenney and Mary Hartley took turns with manuscript drafts.

Special thanks go to Jim Simmons for believing in this story, and to Illinois State Historian Thomas F. Schwartz, and Gordon Pruett for their encouragement.

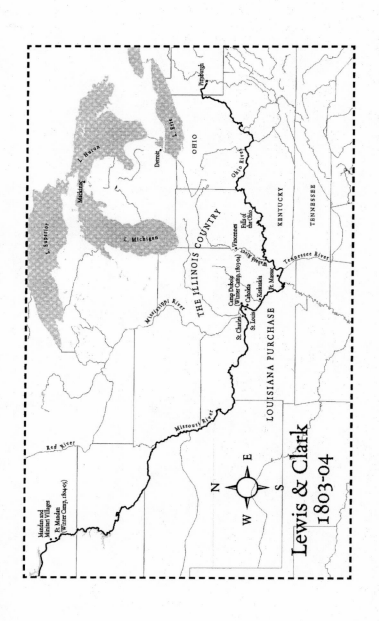

Lewis & Clark
1803-04

1.

A Vast Enterprise

Time spent in the Illinois country by Meriwether Lewis and William Clark during the winter of 1803-04 significantly increased the chances of success for their expedition to the Pacific Ocean. From people in the lightly populated settlements along the western frontier of America, the explorers gathered exhaustive and accurate information that helped meet the challenges of their extraordinary adventure.

Lewis and Clark, accompanied by the men who formed the Corps of Discovery, spent up to six months in or near the Illinois country before they headed up the Missouri River on May 14, 1804. Landing first at Fort Massac on the Ohio River on November 11, 1803, they proceeded to the Mississippi River settlements and eventually to the location of winter camp. Just across the Mississippi from the mouth of the Missouri, the party camped for five months, from December 13, 1803, to May 14, 1804.[1]

Time, however, is a minor point of the story. More important is what Lewis and Clark did during those months, who they met, and how much information they gathered. This is the tale of an expeditionary force to the Pacific forming and shaping on the shores of Illinois, and its interaction with Illinoisans.

An understanding of their activities from November 1803, to May 1804, bolsters the claim that Illinoisans deserved a large measure of credit for success of the expedition, at least as far as the middle Missouri River. A summary of the expedition beginning with its genesis in the mind of Thomas Jefferson provides important background for that conclusion.

Readers of Lewis and Clark expedition history would provide a near-unanimous show of hands to affirm the declaration of Thomas Jefferson as father of a plan to explore the Missouri River and go on to the Pacific Ocean. As a founding father of America and public servant during the nation's early years, Jefferson developed his concept of a western exploration. In the first years of his presidency, 1801 to 1803, Jefferson gave form to the Corps of Discovery, chose the mission and its objectives, obtained congressional approval, and selected leaders capable of meeting the challenges.

As early as 1783, two decades before the Lewis and Clark expedition, Jefferson mused about an exploration of the west in a letter to General George Rogers Clark, the older brother of Captain William Clark. The American Revolution hero politely excused himself from consideration for such a journey.[2] On two other occasions over the years Jefferson encouraged explorers—specifically adventurer John Ledyard and French botanist Andre Michaux—in their ideas for journeys to the Pacific Northwest. Neither succeeded. From these efforts Jefferson's curiosities about the west, as well as political concerns over Pacific Northwest explorations by the British and French, are well established.

As the concept developed in Jefferson's mind, Spanish officials in New Orleans and St. Louis encouraged explorations of the Missouri River in the 1790s. These failed to reach beyond the Mandan Indian villages of today's North Dakota, but they serve as a reminder for students of Lewis and Clark that Americans did not then own exploration rights to the Pacific, nor did the U.S. expedition occur in a vacuum.

Donald Jackson, a Lewis and Clark scholar, wrote that many elements were in play before the Corps of Discovery took shape.

While it is true that Jefferson had since 1783 shown spo-
radic signs that he wanted a transcontinental exploration,
he had done so as a private citizen or as a member of the
American Philosophical Society. During the three years he
served as secretary of state, and four as vice-president, he
had done exactly nothing to press for a government expedition. His purchases of geographical books were minimal.
There is other evidence to consider before we can conclude
that early in 1801, as the new president, he realized that he
would use the power of office to send an exploring team
across the Mississippi.[3]

Jackson says the "other evidence" includes publication in 1801
of Alexander Mackenzie's *Voyages from Montreal* . . . , a memoir of
an exhaustive and heroic journey in 1793 across the Canadian
west. Upon reading of Mackenzie's trek and comments, Jefferson
in 1802 asked for the first appropriation of $2,500 from Congress
for a western exploration. He provided no plan or details.[4] Events
moved quickly after that tentative approach to Congress, propelled
in large part by Jefferson's increasing distrust of the British, and an
extraordinary opportunity to purchase Louisiana country from the
French and Spanish.[5]

Once in the presidency, Jefferson seized the opportunity to
make the expedition a reality. He chose Meriwether Lewis, his
personal secretary and a military veteran, to lead the Corps. Together they selected William Clark of Kentucky as Lewis's partner.
With initial decisions and overtures to Congress made, Jefferson
communicated precise instructions and expectations to Lewis and
Clark. In a lengthy document to Lewis dated June 20, 1803, he
requested information on various scientific subjects, Indians, fur
trade possibilities, climate, mineral production, animals, soil, and
the surest waterways to the Pacific Ocean.

The goal, however, as pronounced in the message by Jefferson,
required just 56 words:

> The object of your mission is to explore the Missouri river,
> & such principal stream of it, as, by it's course and commu-
> nication with the waters of the Pacific ocean, whether the
> Columbia, Oregan, Colorado or any other river may offer
> the most direct & practicable water communication across
> this continent for the purposes of commerce.[6]

Jackson called the president's directions "essential to an understanding of Jefferson's developing attitude toward the West.
They embrace years of study and wonder, the collected wisdom of
his government colleagues and his Philadelphia friends. . . ."[7] Jackson describes Jefferson as excited at the prospect of having specific
information, instead of guesses, about the land beyond the Mississippi. However, it was Clark who found the appropriate words to
describe Jefferson's importance to the expedition. In a letter to
Lewis on July 18, 1803, he said the expedition plan was "Worthey
of that great Chaructor the Main Spring of its action."[8]

Until the Corps of Discovery left Illinois and started up the
Missouri River in May, 1804, Jefferson communicated regularly
with Lewis and expected periodic reports from the captains. However, the president's control over the expedition slipped away almost as soon as Lewis set out on the Ohio River from Pittsburgh.
After Lewis's meeting with William Clark in Indiana Territory, the
communication with Jefferson, with a few exceptions, consisted
mostly of what had happened rather than speculation about the
future. There were instances when Jefferson took exception to plans
of Lewis and Clark, but timing and the vagaries of mail delivery on
the frontier made frequent exchanges over plans impractical.

Well before the party set out to the Pacific Ocean, the two
captains settled into the mode of decision-making that carried
through the expedition and reflected an extraordinary personal
chemistry between them. As equals in the eyes of the men they
commanded, Lewis and Clark shared the responsibilities and decisions that determined the party's fate.

The bond between Lewis and Clark appeared unshakable be-

fore they started together from Clarksville, Indiana Territory, and
it never weakened. Lewis wrote to Clark on June 19, 1803, in his
invitation to join him as co-captain, "If therefore there is anything
under those circumstances, in this enterprise, which would in-
duce you to participate with me in it's fatiegues, it's dangers and
it's honors, believe me there is no man on earth with whom I
should feel equal pleasure in sharing them as with yourself."[9]

Clark returned the compliment in his reply of July 18, saying,
"This is an undertaking fraited with many difficulties, but My
friend I do assure you that no man lives with Whome I would
perfur to undertake Such a Trip &c. as your self."[10]

The argument is sound that the enterprise would not have
succeeded without the combined commitment, wisdom and efforts of the captains, and the sweat of the Corps. Mostly it was an
exemplary voyage—almost too good to be true. It is impossible
not to sit on the edge of the seat as the compelling story unfolds
and the dangers are met and overcome.

The importance of time spent in the Illinois country by Lewis
and Clark has received little attention from historians, thus opening the door to a broader look. Two who have viewed the days in
Illinois in the bigger picture of the enterprise are John Logan Allen
and James Ronda. Allen, in his *Passage Through the Garden: Lewis
and Clark and the Image of the American Northwest,* discusses how
practical information gathered along the Mississippi River collided
with the idealistic, even romantic, view of the West held by Jefferson
and his aides in the east.

Allen writes in detail about the maps and Missouri River travel
journals available to the captains and how they assimilated that
information with impressions brought from the east. He says, "This
means that the more information they gathered in the field, the
more likely they were to reject some of the Jeffersonian concepts."[11]

Allen does not suggest that Lewis and Clark formed totally
new ideas and concepts after arriving in Illinois. He talks more of
the influences and the progressive events that altered the thinking

of Lewis and Clark, adding, "They had enough contacts with knowl-
edgeable persons in St. Louis and on the Illinois side of the Mississippi to indicate that their opinions would probably have been
more linked with the practical frontier experiences and observations" than impressions based on what they heard before arriving
in the Illinois country.[12]

They also carried forward many Jeffersonian ideas along with
their newly gained information. Allen summarized, "Their pre-
conceived notions had an impact on the course of their exploration, on the character of the observations they made, and on the
pattern of beliefs about the geography of the Northwest that came
out of their traverse to the Pacific and back."[13]

Ronda has written extensively of the expedition, especially the
book *Lewis and Clark among the Indians.* He expressed this perspective of the stay in Illinois: "The winter of 1803-04 at Camp
Dubois was more than a time to fit an odd lot of soldiers and
frontiersmen to the discipline Lewis and Clark believed essential
for the expedition's success. The Wood River interlude allowed the
explorers time to gather and evaluate a large amount of information about the Missouri River Indians."[14] That information, Ronda
observed, came from a "crash course" provided by sources available
during the winter.[15]

Ronda believes in a broad interpretation of critical roles in the
expedition. For example, in writing about Lewis and Clark and the
Indians, he emphasizes the importance of good relations with the
Indians to success of the mission. Without the help provided by
Indians from Fort Mandan to the Pacific and back, there might
not have been triumphs to celebrate. More was the reason, Ronda
argues, to obtain the best information possible while in Illinois
about the Indian experiences ahead. A better understanding of the
points made by Allen, Jackson and Ronda comes with a look at
details of the "crash course," and provides evidence to support the
critical role of people in the Illinois country.

When the prelude to the expedition is considered with the hindsight of history, the words of William Clark to Jefferson, written before the journey began, ring loud. In accepting the invitation to accompany Lewis he called the voyage "this Vast enterprise."[16]

2.

The Illinois Country

By the time Lewis and Clark reached the Illinois country for the winter of 1803-04, French, British and American settlers had been around for more than a century. For generations before that, Indian tribes hunted and gathered in the land of prairies, lakes, rivers and rolling timberland. What eventually became the heartland and breadbasket of the United States had served natives and settlers comfortably for centuries, with only an occasional encroachment of progress and turmoil.

After the American Revolution, in the 1780s, the federal government and thirteen original states began thinking about the land west to the Mississippi River and how it should be divided into territories and eventually into states. The Illinois country first was organized as part of a large area known as the Northwest Territory that stretched from the Ohio River to the border with Canada, and from Ohio to the Mississippi. That division lasted until roughly 1800 when the western portion of Northwest Territory was established as Indiana Territory. In the time of Lewis and Clark, Indiana Territory included all of what is now the state of Illinois. The smaller Territory of Illinois was formed in 1809.

Indiana Territory stretched over a huge portion of the Midwest and through the Mississippi River and Ohio River valleys. William Henry Harrison, governor of Indiana Territory and future

U.S. president, used Vincennes, now in Indiana along the Wabash River, as headquarters. The youthful Harrison—still in his 20s—was years away from his triumphant victory over Indians at Tippecanoe, and his brief tenure as president of the United States in 1841. His name and correspondence are among documents directly relating to the Lewis and Clark adventure, indicating he may have learned of the expedition from President Jefferson. Also, William Clark and the governor knew each other and corresponded before and during the Corps' winter in the Illinois country.

The eastern boundary of Harrison's domain began at the mouth of the Kentucky River on the Ohio midway between Louisville and Cincinnati at Carrollton, Kentucky, and went north to Fort Recovery, about 25 miles beyond Greenville, Ohio, on the border with Indiana. The boundary continued due north from Fort Recovery to Canada. The Mississippi River formed the western boundary of the territory.[1] East of the line lay the present state of Ohio, a small piece of southeastern Indiana between the mouth of the Kentucky and the Great Miami rivers, the eastern half of the lower peninsula of Michigan and the eastern tip of the upper peninsula.

Based on population counts taken in the 1800 census, fewer than 6,000 white residents lived in Indiana Territory.[2] About 2,500 of those resided within the borders of present-day Illinois. The census reported 929 people on George Rogers Clark's land grant on the Ohio; 714 at Vincennes; and 600 at various Great Lakes posts. In Illinois the census counted 719 at Cahokia; 467 at Kaskaskia; 212 at Prairie du Rocher between Cahokia and Kaskaskia; 250 along the southern border of St. Clair County; 334 in scattered parts of Monroe County, and about 90 at Fort Massac. Peoria was the only other Illinois location showing up in the census with 100 people. The population of the Illinois country hardly had grown in 50 years.

Moreover, other than locations along the Mississippi River, the land was inhospitable and dangerous. No roads existed. Congress first appropriated money to construct a series of roads in Indiana Territory in 1806, but work did not begin until years

later. Thick timber and wild rivers and creeks restricted any kind
of movement in southernmost Illinois. Winds swept the vast, barren prairies.

To travel from Vincennes on the Wabash River to Kaskaskia on
the Mississippi River required more than 40 hours on horseback
through forests and over prairies covered in summer with thick
grasses 10 to 12 feet high, and in winter open to the wind and
snows that swept down from the north. On a present-day map of
Illinois it is possible to draw distinctive lines describing the landscape of 1803. Below a line drawn from Rock Island to Peoria and
on to Champaign-Urbana, mixed woodlands and prairies prevailed.
Southernmost Illinois was woodlands and rolling hills. To the north
of the line stretched prairies as far as the eye could see.

An enduring description of the southern Illinois landscape,
and the hazards of overland travel, appears in the account by John
Reynolds of his family's trek from a point near Fort Massac to
Kaskaskia in 1800. Reynolds, a child at the time, became a distinguished citizen of Illinois, serving in Congress and as governor.
Late in life he wrote recollections of early Illinois days in a pioneer
history of the state. Reynolds estimated the journey at 110 miles—
others use the 140-mile estimate for the trail—zig-zagging "through
the wilderness." It took the family four weeks to make the "dreary
and desolate journey."[3]

Reynolds's family encountered the aftermath of a tornado that
had blown down timber and filled the trail with trunks and
branches. They had to cut a new trail around the toppled trees.
The swollen Big Muddy River proved a major obstacle. The family
built a raft after waiting for the river level to fall, and was forced to
"swim the horses." About the animals, he said, "The horses became poor, for the want of grain, or grass." They rafted the less
dangerous Little Muddy creek, also running high because of spring
rains. They eventually made it to Kaskaskia without further difficulty.

Dr. George Hunter, a physician and druggist from the eastern
U.S., traveled overland in Illinois in 1796 keeping a journal which
provided another recorded experience in southern Illinois. Enroute

from Vincennes to Kaskaskia his party lost its way and suffered
various discomforts, including lack of water, droves of mosquitoes
and gnats, horseflies "as large as the largest bumble bee," prairie
grass and weeds that rose "two or three feet higher than a man on
horseback."[4] It got so hot one night in camp that Hunter stripped
himself naked "expecting to inhale the dew by the pores of my
skin but was so terribly pestered by the bite of the mosquetos that
I was soon obliged to cover myself with my blanket. . . ."

The land and its obstacles frightened early settlers, but over
time travelers to the Illinois country waxed eloquent about the
beauty of the woodlands in the south and the prairies to the north.
One visitor described the countryside as "the touching, delicate
loveliness of the lesser prairies, so resplendent in brilliancy of hue
and beauty of outline."[5] The point of view often depended on the
experience during travel.

Early newcomers to the Illinois country used the water route
in spite of its dangers. Settlers from Kentucky and Tennessee often
chose a flatboat for floating down the Ohio. Those who decided to
continue on the water then sailed and poled against the current on
the Mississippi until landing somewhere along the flood plain
between Kaskaskia and Cahokia, the two earliest and largest settlements. Eventually a popular migration route combined a flatboat
on the Ohio to a point in the Illinois country near present-day
Golconda. Some people stopped on the Kentucky side and took a
ferry to Illinois. The remainder of the journey to Kaskaskia or
Cahokia continued overland through southern Illinois.[6]

As settlers made their way up the Mississippi with Spanish-
held Louisiana on the left and the Illinois country on the right,
they traveled alongside and camped on one of the most fertile
areas of Illinois, indeed the nation, called the American Bottom.
This stretch of historic Mississippi River flood plain is where the
great tribes of early Indians made their homes and built giant
mounds. French life flourished along the Bottom from the late
1600s through 1760 before being joined by people from England

and the colonies. By Lewis and Clark's time many Americans had arrived to make their mark on the soil.

The Bottom stretches from south of where the Kaskaskia River enters the Mississippi, near Chester, for 70 miles northward near Alton. In contrast, on the western side of the river huge stands of trees and high bluffs hid Louisiana country from river view, and provided no such strip of productive land. Illinois settlers had easy access to the river with high bluffs set back from the river, cutting off the flood plain from the prairies.[7] Alvord wrote of the American Bottom, "Little wonder that this small strip of territory has become the most historic in all the state."[8]

The population of the American Bottom was concentrated in the small settlements of Kaskaskia, Cahokia, Prairie du Rocher and Bellefontaine. From Cahokia northward only a scattered few individual pioneers lived. Native Americans also roamed the Bottom and nearby. By 1803 they were peaceful, but the days of open hostility with whites would return.

Prolific animal life in the Bottom attracted early settlers, and provided an accessible food source to supplement farming. The field notes of William Clark, written while the expedition wintered on the Wood River north of Cahokia, describe repeated hunting excursions by soldiers and a proliferation of game. Backwaters, lakes, streams, and the oak and hickory forests of the flood plain provided mussels, fish, turtles, birds and mammals. Game included elk, black bear, and bobcat. Beaver, mink, muskrat and river otter inhabited the waters. During certain seasons huge numbers of ducks, geese, swans, and wading birds migrated along the Mississippi flyway.[9]

Travelers through the American Bottom before 1800 took special note of the beauty and bounty. Dr. Hunter described the American Bottom near Prairie du Rocher in his journal.

> The Timber upon the high Country is light & placed very
> far apart not unlike an orchard where the trees are planted at
> a great distance apart, in order that they may cultivate the

ground in the intermediate spaces. The Grass grows here,
very long, & this upland meadow altho at least 150 feet
above the Meadows on the banks of the Missisipi yeilds
very good grass & a great quantity of it.[10]

Moses Austin, touring Illinois in 1797 on his way to establish
a colony in Texas, offered this view on the subject:

> The Illinois Country is perhaps one of the most Beautifull
> and fertile in America and has the perculiar advantage of
> beeing interspersed with large plains or prairies and Wood
> Lands, where a Crop can be made the first year, without the
> trouble and Expence of falling the timber, which in every
> other part of America exhaust the strenght and purse of a
> New Settler.[11]

Proving that no place is perfect, residents and visitors often
complained of the weather, humidity, heat and mosquitoes near
the water sources. Malaria was common. Floods provided the most
unpleasant aspect of life in the American Bottom. Before levees
were constructed many decades later, portions of the plain flooded
annually and in some years water covered most of the Bottom.

The French first settled outposts along the Bottom, farmed
the productive land, co-existed with Indian tribes, established an
enduring culture and watched as the English and then Americans
overtook them. In this regard, the story of Bellefontaine is one of
the intriguing tales of American frontier settlement that holds a
special place in Illinois history relating to the American Bottom
and the resident French. The memory of Bellefontaine stands even
today as a shining example of American ingenuity, impetuosity,
and political courage.[12]

While the American Revolution raged in 1779 a small band of
Americans from Virginia and Maryland left the chaos of the eastern seaboard for Kentucky. They heard from George Rogers Clark
and his frontier soldiers about the richness of Illinois soil and the

pleasant environment of river bottomlands. Although non-French settlements were forbidden north of the Ohio River, the Americans went anyway to see the Mississippi Valley for themselves, bringing the first Anglo-Saxon names to Illinois. As historian Robert Howard wrote, they provided the land along the Mississippi its name: The American Bottom.[13]

The Americans found an ideal settlement location along a creek between Prairie du Rocher and Cahokia just south of the present city of Waterloo. All was not peaceful, however. American settlers chafed under French rule. Flexing their independence, Americans did what they wanted without regard for French customs or laws. The French did not think much of the troublesome Americans, and complained that the newcomers encroached on their property and riled the Indians by providing them liquor. Officials feared violence between the rambunctious Americans and the normally passive French.

Cahokia residents came to the rescue by offering to include Bellefontaine in its jurisdiction, and allowing Americans to elect their own local judges. Apparently the Americans preferred the French in Cahokia to the French in Kaskaskia. The residents of Bellefontaine ceased their saber rattling and settled down in Cahokia jurisdiction. By the time of Lewis and Clark there were about 300 residents in the Bellefontaine community.[14]

The first Frenchmen—Louis Jolliet and Jacques Marquette—stopped on the shores near the confluence of the Missouri and Mississippi rivers in 1673, the date when written history begins for Illinois. Priests of the Seminary of Quebec established Holy Family mission at Cahokia in 1699, the same year as the founding of Williamsburg, Virginia, marking that lonesome Illinois location as the first white settlement on the Mississippi River.[14] Slowly, French settlers came to the region and the town site. Inhabitants tended to be transients, traders with resident Indians who roamed the Mississippi Valley in small groups, and an occasional settler. Few early records of Cahokia have been preserved, so full accounts of the first decades are lacking.

The first recorded population estimate of the Illinois country, probably less than accurate, occurred in 1723. It revealed seven white inhabitants of Cahokia. By comparison, Fort de Chartres, the lone French military and trade post in Illinois country, had a population of 126, and 196 people lived in Kaskaskia. This and other early population counts included Indian and Negro slaves among the settlers. A count in 1752 indicated Cahokia's population had risen to 136.[15]

In similar fashion, Kaskaskia, Cahokia's twin settlement on the Mississippi, began in 1703. The Kaskaskia Indians migrated to the place where the Kaskaskia River flowed into the Mississippi just above the present city of Chester. Father Pierre Gabriel Marest, a French Jesuit priest, accompanied the Indians. Soon missionaries, colonists, explorers, and traders joined them.[16] The American Bottom settlement site of Kaskaskia provided water access to the fur trade of New Orleans and the Upper Mississippi, productive soils, and a relatively pleasant environment. Kaskaskia developed a unique brand of French charm, and became known as "the Paris of the west."

Kaskaskia's glory days came and went over time, with one of the highlights being the period of territorial government from 1809 to statehood in 1818, when Kaskaskia was the seat of government. First officials of the state, meeting in Kaskaskia, chose Vandalia in southern Illinois as the permanent capital beginning in 1819, and the slow, agonizing decline of Kaskaskia accelerated.[17]

The final chapter of Kaskaskia began amid heavy snows north of Illinois and formation of huge ice fields on the Mississippi below St. Louis in the winter of 1880-81, endangering the community. These forces and the changing channel of the Mississippi River over the next two decades caused the eventual erosion of Kaskaskia village. By 1910 nothing remained of Kaskaskia. Changes in the Mississippi River course and the mouth of the Kaskaskia River have cut Kaskaskia "island" off from the Illinois mainland. Now the nearest Illinois town to the previous island of Kaskaskia is Chester.

Kaskaskia and Cahokia developed separately and quietly, while

competing for status in trade. Eventually, the two became quarrel-
some rivals, providing the issues and animosities that led to the
first political arguments in Illinois history. But during the early
decades Kaskaskia and Cahokia grew slowly and remained relatively content, given the deprivations and solitude of frontier life.
This lasted until conflict between England and France in the French
and Indian War, and the development of St. Louis just a ferry ride
across the Mississippi from Cahokia.[18]

The French and Indian tribes in the vicinity co-existed without major conflict from the early days of settlement before 1700,
and there seemed no special reason to fortify the eastern side of the
Mississippi with several military outposts. The French built one
fort, called Fort de Chartres, just north of Kaskaskia between the
two major settlements.

The French built the first Fort de Chartres in 1720 about a
half-mile from the Mississippi and 19 miles north of Kaskaskia. It
provided protection from hostile Indians, and served as a post for
Mississippi River trade and French administration. That fort lasted
about five years. After floodwaters endangered the wooden structure, the French built a second fort of log walls further from the
river. A series of inept commanders and a lack of maintenance
brought the second fort to ruin in 1748. At that point the French
garrison moved to a temporary fort near Kaskaskia.

The French did not give up on having a fort at the old location. For the third facility they used limestone for the walls, and
took occupancy in 1754. Meanwhile, the British and French were
engaged in the French and Indian War. Soldiers from Fort de
Chartres were dispatched to distant points in Canada to battle the
British, but the war did not reach the Illinois country.

The British vanquished the French in 1765. Shortly thereafter
British troops arrived at Fort de Chartres, displacing French soldiers. The British changed the installation's name to Fort Cavendish,
but did little beyond that. A series of lackluster commanders came
and went, and many of the nearby French residents left to join the
founders of St. Louis across the river. By 1771 the British, frus-

trated in trying to govern the Illinois country by long distance, walked away from Fort de Chartres and provided no other form of security for settlers. Only the ruins of the fort remained when William Clark visited the region in 1797 on a mission for his brother George Rogers.

On the heels of British victories at forts Duquesne, Quebec and Montreal in 1763, France gave up in North America and ceded its lands to England, ushering in a period of extreme unhappiness and dislocation among French settlers. Almost simultaneously, Pierre Laclede Liguest and his young stepson, Auguste Chouteau, chose the site for a new village on the west side of the Mississippi across from Cahokia. St. Louis was born.[19] Laclede, a native of France, arrived in New Orleans in 1755 and eight years later went up the Mississippi in search of a location for a trading post. Near the mouth of the Missouri River he chose the spot in Louisiana Territory, and with Chouteau became the first citizens of St. Louis.

With all the turmoil, Cahokia and Kaskaskia dwindled in population. The Illinois country meant little to the British except for its role in trade north of the Ohio River and as a buffer to prevent the Spanish from expanding their interests. The Spanish cared not at all about the Illinois country, and recruited French settlers from the Illinois country with offers of free land. In this unsettled environment leading to 1800, the village of St. Louis grew steadily. With the flight of people from Illinois, St. Louis became a community of predominantly French people on Spanish soil. By 1798, the population of St. Louis was estimated at 800, and had climbed close to 1,000 when Lewis and Clark arrived.

St. Louis was a dramatic contrast to the Illinois settlements, which added to the desirability of living there. Mississippi Valley historian John Francis McDermott described St. Louis as a planned city, not an accidental growth around a mission and not a gathering place of frontiersmen, such as Cahokia and Kaskaskia.[20] The community was a commercial center and seat of government. At the time of Lewis and Clark, St. Louis also had become the center of Mississippi Valley trade with goods moving down to New Orleans, and up river to the Illinois and Missouri rivers and trade centers further north. Given their history, attitudes and governance problems, Kaskaskia and Cahokia could not compete with the rise of St. Louis.

During the 1790s, a fresh migration to Kaskaskia and Cahokia of fur traders and land speculators, some French and some Americans, revived the two communities slightly. The damage had been done, however. St. Louis dominated life and business in the region. Lewis and Clark discovered the reality of competition between Illinois and St. Louis soon after they arrived. But they also learned that people in the Illinois settlements had accumulated knowledge and experience that could help them prepare for the Missouri River journey.

3.

The First Clark

There should have been a drum roll or the sound of trumpets when Lewis and Clark met at Clarksville along the Ohio River in Indiana Territory on October 15, 1803. They had seen one another in recent years but only recently had exchanged correspondence about the expedition, started in June by Lewis.[1] They shared each other's lives for the next three years, and remained inseparable for all time in the nation's most celebrated exploration.

From the beginning, in Washington deliberations and Pittsburgh where the water journey started, Lewis recognized the importance of having a strong, and familiar, colleague to provide co-leadership. When the captains met and got down to business, their extraordinary personal chemistry began to influence the excursion. They had a remarkable friendship, and it made for a memorable journey.

Virtually nothing is known in the captains' words about their meeting near the foot of the rapids called the falls of the Ohio, or the two weeks they spent together before heading on down the Ohio River in a keelboat and two canoe-like pirogues.[2] Lewis's journal contained no entries regarding the meeting.

Not far from the river William Clark lived with his older brother (by 18 years), General George Rogers Clark, famed Revolutionary War hero of the western front. The general, who knew the Illinois country and Indiana Territory well, probably was present for some of the discussions between Lewis and Clark. Perhaps they talked over good food and drink, and listened to George Rogers reminisce about the general's experiences in the Illinois country.

While Lewis brought Clark up to date on the planned excursion and his difficult experiences and delays in getting started, a highlight of their talks would have been conversations about the mysteries of the Far West. Conversation would have flowed easily because of an instant camaraderie among them, based on a shared military background. Although General Clark, age 51, had far more experiences on which to draw, the knowledge that all had served as army officers provided a basis for conversation. It did not hurt, either, that all three had family roots in Virginia.

George Rogers Clark played a significant role in the history that laid groundwork for the Lewis and Clark journey. He left footsteps throughout the Illinois country, from Fort Massac on the Ohio River to Kaskaskia and Cahokia, and back across what is now the state of Illinois to Vincennes. Historian Alvord called George Rogers Clark "inseparably connected with Illinois history."[3]

George Rogers was in his 26th year—about the age of William during his service in the U.S. army—when his military adventures in the Illinois country began. The initial saga covered 14 months from inception at Williamsburg, Virginia, late in 1777, to climax at Fort Sackville near Vincennes, early in 1779. Clark and the frontier soldiers who followed him changed the face of the American Revolution in the west.

Clark feared no one. A charismatic leader, and unflappable under fire, he proved also to be a brilliant strategist. He bore a striking resemblance to George Washington, which added to his luster. Never one to hide his activities under a rock, Clark many years later called himself one of "the first and last of the officers who bore the weight of that war."[4]

Late in 1777, Clark laid a plan before Governor Patrick Henry of Virginia to recruit a force of frontier soldiers to march on and capture the French settlements of Kaskaskia and Cahokia on the Mississippi River, which at that time were under nominal governance of the British. Recognizing an opportunity for Virginia to extend its influence westward, Henry bought the idea and permitted Clark, then with the rank of lieutenant colonel, to find upwards of 175 soldiers in Kentucky. Friends and foes alike across the Ohio River basin eventually knew them as "The Long Knives."

After recruiting and equipping his army, Clark led the party down the Ohio River to Fort Massac, a military installation abandoned by the British. The site is now located in an Illinois state park near the town of Metropolis. The army rested a day at the site of Fort Massac and obtained the services of a hunter who recently had left Kaskaskia and who presumably knew the overland route to the settlement. Then Clark and his soldiers began the trek over inhospitable countryside.[5] Clark needed to move quickly and quietly to capitalize on the element of surprise.

Clark led his troops on a march of 140 miles on a southern Illinois route that cut through heavy timber and along and across creeks and rivers that often overflowed. Swamps dotted the landscape. Four days after leaving Massac, the hunter lost his way and food supplies had dwindled. He finally got his bearings—after a tongue-lashing from Clark—and in two more days, on July 4, 1778, the party reached Kaskaskia.[6] Clark took the settlement—which had no military security—without firing a shot, and captured the British agent, Philip Rocheblave.[7]

Gabriel Cerre, a newcomer to Kaskaskia who later became a celebrated fur trader and businessman, left Kaskaskia on business before Clark arrived, but his wife had a memorable encounter with the colonel. Sixty-eight years later their son, Pashal Leon Cerre, a child in 1778, recalled the episode involving Clark and his mother at the Cerre home.[8]

Pashal said Clark arrived quietly on a moonlit night. With no opposing British forces in the region, he went to the home of Cerre and looked through the window for signs of Gabriel. "Madam Cerre with indignation seized the poker, after jumping out of bed, threatening to break his head." Clark explained that he intended no harm, and she gave him permission to look for her husband.

Clark checked under the bed with a candle and then withdrew, without disturbing the children.

Sometime later at a dinner given by the Spanish governor in St. Louis, Clark and Gabriel Cerre met each other. "Clark politely begged to drink a glass with M. Cerre, who said, 'Yes, Col. Clark, we can touch our glasses in friendship, and I am glad that circumstances have so brought it about; but, Sir, had I been at home when you searched under the bed for me at Kaskaskia, we should not both have been here now!'"

After securing Kaskaskia, Clark dispatched his second in command, Captain Joseph Bowman, on a mission northward along the Mississippi River flood plain to capture French villages, including Cahokia. Bowman moved quickly. Without firing a shot he occupied Prairie du Rocher, Cahokia, and a few other small settlements. Clark and Bowman had taken the Illinois country in the name of America. Clark immediately set up administrative operations and allowed for the election of judges. He began a series of peace talks with Indian tribes.[9]

Governor Henry exulted in Clark's capture of the Illinois country and efforts to make peace with nearby Indians, probably because it gave impetus to Virginia's imperial ambitions. On December 9, 1778, Virginia officials formally annexed the Illinois country then instructed Clark to consider taking Detroit.[10] That may have been easy for the Virginians to say, but the order failed to consider the reality of Clark's situation.

Clark first had to secure his tenuous hold on the Illinois country. If he miscalculated the military situation, his soldiers faced certain failure and probable defeat. Clark had no means of providing for his frontier soldiers and they soon grew weary of the duty and wanted to leave for home. Clark also knew the British would hear of his conquest and begin plotting to move troops into the Illinois country and reclaim the settlements. Clark's small band of 175 soldiers could not hold out long against superior British forces, supplemented by hundreds of friendly Indians. Clark expected the British to move on Cahokia and Kaskaskia no later than the following spring. He eliminated the option of marching on the military stronghold of Detroit, but still faced the immediate problem of caring for his soldiers.

Charles Gratiot, a Cahokia-based trader, came to the immediate aid of the Americans. In 1777 Gratiot opened a Cahokia store and established a thriving trade business with the British and friendly Indians. Talkative and gregarious, Gratiot quickly became a leading citizen. The native of Switzerland proclaimed loyalty to the revolution and to Clark, and followed that with action. He knew that French farmers in the area could not provide adequate food and shelter without leadership, and he understood that the government in Virginia could not provide relief soon. Gratiot, who twenty-two years later played a sizable role in preparations for Lewis and Clark's expedition, took the initiative to acquire food and provisions for the soldiers, knowing he might never be repaid.[11]

This generosity put Gratiot at considerable risk. If Clark failed and the British overran Illinois, Gratiot would be among the first civilian targets because of his partisanship. Also by favoring the Americans, Gratiot put his fur trade operations in jeopardy in Canada and England. Word traveled fast on the highly competitive trade circuit. Still, Gratiot did not hesitate to help.

Meanwhile Henry Hamilton, lieutenant governor of Detroit, heard of Clark's victories and began planning a British counterattack, in effect setting up one of American history's classic high-stakes military confrontations in the western theater. Hamilton's deputy on the mission to defeat Clark was Jehu Hay, whose son John later became a distinguished citizen of Cahokia and close associate of William Clark and Meriwether Lewis. Jehu Hay had responsibility for recruiting Indian tribes to accompany the British. Hay knew the Indians well in his role as Hamilton's agent to reward the warriors for harassing American settlers.

Hamilton's first step toward finding and capturing Clark and his soldiers was to seize Fort Sackville at Vincennes, then controlled by the French. In December, 1778, about 100 British soldiers joined by approximately 500 Indians recruited by Hay crossed the icy wilderness from Lake Erie to the Maumee River, and took the Wabash River to Vincennes, a trek of 600 miles.[12] After seizing the fort without a fight, Hamilton had to decide whether to press on to Cahokia and engage Clark in the dead of winter, or wait in Vincennes for more favorable conditions. Fatefully, Hamilton decided to remain and strengthen the works at Fort Sackville before pursuing Clark in the spring.

Back in the Illinois country, Clark conferred with officers and concluded that victory depended on the success of a winter surprise attack on Fort Sackville. Spies, including frontiersman Simon Kenton and Clark associate Shadrach Bond, Sr., both of whom surface again in this story, returned from a reconnaissance to Vincennes with encouraging reports about opportunities for a surprise attack to succeed.[13]

Little more than a week after hearing of Hamilton's success at Vincennes, Clark assembled 130 Long Knives and a few Frenchmen, and left Kaskaskia on foot for Vincennes.[14] The trek eastward across Illinois made the earlier march from Fort Massac to Kaskaskia seem like a picnic. Rains had swollen the creeks and rivers of the region, inundating already swampy land. There was no guarantee they could march 150 miles to Vincennes without being detected. Bands of Indians roamed the prairie and at any moment could have scuttled Clark's plan. The soldiers, with little food, suffered greatly. They slept in the cold and wet and often marched in water up to their necks. Clark motivated the men by reminding them of the atrocities Indians had committed on settlers with encouragement of Governor Hamilton.

While Hamilton, Jehu and their confederates waited until spring for an offensive, Clark and his soldiers marched secretly to Fort Sackville where Clark forced the surrender of Hamilton in one of America's most dramatic moments of the war. During negotiations for the surrender, Clark encountered Jehu Hay for the first time. Obviously Clark knew of Jehu's reputation for carrying out Hamilton's orders with the Indians, and the American officer did not think much of it.

Clark insisted on unconditional surrender during negotiations with Hamilton and Jehu, although the British held out for certain conditions. This led to protracted discussions. In his memoir, Clark provides his version of one heated exchange after Hamilton's resistance to Clark's terms.[15]

Clark told Hamilton he was prepared to fight to the death, "that the Cries of the Widows and Fatherless on the Frontiers that they had occationed now Required their Blood from my Hands. . . ." Clark said if Hamilton chose to risk the massacre of his garrison "for their stakes it was at his own pleasure and that I perhaps might take it in my head to send for some of those Widows to see it Executed." Clark decried the British as "Indian partizans."

Clark wrote that he saw "Maj. Hay paying great attention. I had observed a kind of distrust in his countenance which in a great measure influenced my Conversation during this time." Hamilton asked Clark, who is it that you call "Indian partizans?" Clark replied, "Sir . . . I take Maj. Hay to be one of the Principals." Then Clark added, "I never saw a man in the Moment of Execution So Struck as he appeared to be Pail and Trembling scarcely able to stand."[16]

The image of Hay, a fearless combatant and proud soldier, cowering at the table raises questions about the account. Nevertheless, Jehu may well have been concerned for his life. Hamilton acknowledged fear of violence at the hands of their captors, and there is reason to believe British soldiers did not hold Jehu in high regard either. Jehu completed his duties at the surrender by writing out the final terms for signature by the principals.[17]

Clark dispatched Hamilton, Jehu and 24 associates to prison in Williamsburg, Virginia. Hay wrote nothing about his time in prison, but Hamilton complained bitterly about his treatment at the hands of American partisans in a report he filed after being released. Twice American officials offered Hamilton and Hay opportunities for parole, and twice they turned them down, saying the conditions were unreasonable and could not be met. Finally, on a third attempt, the parties agreed to a parole and exchange for American prisoners held by the British.[18]

The surprise victory of Clark's smaller numbers over Hamilton's force at the Fort completed one of the most improbable tales of the American Revolution, and put the Illinois country on the strategic map. Clark became a hero and never-forgotten military leader, although subsequent battles did not end as successfully. By protecting American settlements along the Mississippi, Clark set the stage for an expedition that included his brother William to form on shores of the Illinois country two decades later.

George Rogers Clark surfaced in the history of the Corps of Discovery on at least two occasions before his brother William joined Meriwether Lewis, when the general and Thomas Jefferson corresponded about an expedition to explore the west. The first occurred as Jefferson re-entered public life on the rebound following a nearly disastrous experience as governor of Virginia. After accepting a position as delegate to the Continental Congress, Jefferson for the first time put some of his thoughts about exploring the west in correspondence with General Clark. In Jefferson's letter of December 4, 1783, he wrote of England's interest in exploring the country beyond the Mississippi River to California. Curious about how the English might be stopped, Jefferson asked of Clark: "How would you like to lead such a party?"[19]

Responding from Richmond, Virginia, Clark recognized Jefferson's offer as a gesture of respect, but declined to lead an expedition. "Your proposition respecting a tour to the west and North west of the Continent would be Extreamly agreable. . . ." if it were not for the reality of Clark's poor financial condition. "Should Congress risolve to have the western Country Explored I should take pleasure in lending all the aid in my power as an Individual. It is what I think we ought to do."[20]

While withdrawing from consideration, Clark had his own opinion about how such an exploration should be organized and conducted. It is instructive to view George Rogers' approach toward exploring unfriendly and unknown territory. "Large parties will never answer the purpose. They will allarm the Indian Nations they pass through. Three or four young Men well qualified for the Task might perhaps compleat your wishes at a very Trifling Expence." He failed to see that a large party would be essential for a lengthy expedition, but his estimate of four or five years to complete the task was close to the target.

The second contact between George Rogers Clark and Jefferson occurred in 1802, about six months before Lewis left the east on the journey. George Rogers wrote President Jefferson about finding a government job for his younger brother. It is possible the general knew Jefferson had expedition plans, but it is unlikely the president would have shared them with the general at that early stage.

From his home on the falls of the Ohio River, General Clark wrote Jefferson offering the services of William, and agreeing to help him in any way:

> I have long since laid aside all Idea of Public affairs, by bad fortune, and ill health. I have become incapable of persuing those enterpriseing & active persuits which I have been fond of from my youth—but I will with the greatest pleasure give my bro. William every information in my power on this, or any other point which may be of Service to your Administration. He is well quallified almost for any business. If it should be in your power to confur on him any post of Honor and profit, in this Countrey in which we live, it will exceedingly gratify me. . . . [21]

4.

Lewis and Clark: Frontiersmen

Meriwether Lewis and William Clark were not strangers who just happened to end up serving on the same expedition to the Pacific Ocean. They had a brief history together during service in the military in the early 1790s. Prior to an invitation from Lewis to Clark in 1803 to join him on the journey they had spent time together in Washington, D.C. Clark made trips to the capital in 1800, 1801 and 1802 when he met with Lewis and became acquainted with President Jefferson. Additionally, their years on the frontier of early America, and especially the journeys of William Clark, provide a meaningful backdrop to the adventure in the Illinois country.

Lewis, age 29 when the expedition began, had years of experience roaming the wilderness of the Ohio Valley, the region south of the Ohio River, and his home state of Virginia. No stranger to military life, Lewis had seen the dangers of the frontier and understood the challenges of sparsely settled country. Still, Lewis had not engaged directly in fighting Indians or the British. He had, at the most, five years of experience away from his home territory and family in Virginia.[1]

Lewis got his first taste of military life in 1794 as a 20-year-old volunteer in the Virginia militia. He answered President George Washington's call for thousands of volunteers to quell protests by

American citizens in the wilderness west over taxes on whiskey made on the frontier, which became known as the Whiskey Rebellion.[2] Americans had an historic sensitivity to being excessively taxed, and they objected strenuously to taxes on whiskey made on the frontier. Lewis participated in the rout of rebels without exchanging gunfire.

After militia service Lewis received a commission as ensign in the regular army and an assignment to serve with troops of General Anthony Wayne, the first military leader in the Northwest Territory to defeat Indians in large-scale battle. Wayne had attained hero status before Lewis joined his army with a victory near present-day Toledo, Ohio, at the battle of Fallen Timbers. The triumph turned the tide for American settlers who had lived at the mercy of hostile Indians since the revolution.

Lewis's army experience hit bottom in 1795 when a fellow officer charged him with drunkenness and with challenging the officer to a duel.[3] Challenging a fellow soldier to a duel in the frontier army did not constitute a crime in the eyes of officers. On the contrary, those who refused to accept the challenge often were penalized. In this context, a court martial absolved Lewis of guilt. But afterward Lewis could not serve with the aggrieved soldier and commanders reassigned Lewis. This twist of fate brought Lewis and Clark together.

Lewis's transfer put him in the Chosen Rifle Company of sharpshooters based at Fort Greenville, in what is now the far southwest corner of Ohio. Lieutenant William Clark commanded the company.[4] Although there is no account available of the meeting, they could not avoid some level of familiarity in a small company of men. Even so, their association was brief because on September 10, 1795, Clark left Fort Greenville on a special mission for General Wayne and by the end of the year he took an extended leave. Clark's biographer believes the path with Lewis crossed either in the summer of 1795 or more likely at the beginning of 1796 after Clark's mission for General Wayne.[5]

Another chance meeting dating to the frontier army of Anthony Wayne had implications for Lewis and Clark less than a decade later. William Henry Harrison, a Virginian who was a year older than Lewis and three years younger than Clark, held a position of trust with the commanding general. Harrison served as aide-de-camp to Wayne during the victory over Indians at Fallen Timbers. After that battle, when Lewis joined Wayne's army, the three were within a few miles of each other. Following a promotion to captain in 1798, Harrison left the military and entered the arena of territorial politics. Two years later President John Adams named him governor of Indiana Territory.

Lewis continued serving in Wayne's army, making reconnaissance missions north and south of the Ohio River in Northwest Territory. In 1799 he was posted as a recruiter in Charlottesville, Virginia, and later became an army paymaster. These positions required him to travel extensively along the Atlantic seaboard and to the south on administrative missions. He went to work as President Jefferson's secretary in 1801.[6] This career move put him in position to be on the front pages of American exploration history.

One way to examine the extent of Lewis's experience on the frontier is to view it on a map of the United States. During his years with Wayne's army, Lewis had an opportunity to see much of the countryside east of the current boundary between Indiana and Ohio. The territory between Virginia and Ohio was familiar to him also. This knowledge provided a basis for understanding the western wilderness. Nevertheless, Lewis had no command experience.

Born August 1, 1770, William Clark accompanied his father John and family from Virginia to Kentucky and settled at a place called "Mulberry Hill" in 1786. The ninth of ten children, William had five older brothers and three sisters.[7] At that time Kentucky contained the largest American population of any state or territory on the far western frontier. Settlers lived dangerously in constant fear of deadly encounters with Indian tribes from north of the Ohio River who wanted to keep whites south of the river. As Kentuckians pushed across the Ohio River to claim Indian lands, the tribes pushed back, often resulting in deaths on both sides. In response George Rogers Clark organized Kentucky frontiersmen to fight the Indians. It is possible that William joined in some of the raids although there is no record of his participation.

Those who chronicled William Clark's early years in Kentucky describe him as physically large and strong. He spent much of his youth honing skills as a hunter, horseman and woodsman. When military action took shape to counter the Indian threat, he volunteered and accepted responsibility for protecting Kentucky interests. With the exception of the years 1796 to 1803 when he farmed in Kentucky, Clark was a military or civil servant until his death in 1838. William's first known military experience occurred in 1789, at age 19, as a member of Major John Hardin's militia that moved across the Ohio to pursue Indians. On his excursion with Hardin, Clark kept a daily journal noting distances and routes of the march. He described the Ohio as "the beutifullest river I ever saw."[8]

We know from accounts of the Lewis and Clark expedition that Clark was the most dutiful, if not the most flamboyant, journal writer of the co-captains. The essential characteristic of Clark's field notes and journals to and from the Pacific was a terse recording of data, little elaboration or detail, and a tendency for creative spelling. He came by the inclination to keep an expedition journal naturally, as shown by records of his military service during the 1790s. He first demonstrated the writing style with Hardin's militia, and again in 1794 with General Wayne's army in the battle of Fallen Timbers.[9]

The next military excursion involving Clark occurred in 1791 when he joined about 800 soldiers on a mission under command of Brigadier General Charles Scott to rout Indians on the Wabash River. After the troops cleared Indians from the region, Clark joined the army of General Wayne, with headquarters at Fort Greenville. Lieutenant Clark made the long march with Wayne's troops to battle Indians at Fallen Timbers. He kept a diary of events, including harsh criticism of General Wayne's strategies and handling of troops.[10] Clark remained with Wayne in garrison duty for nearly a year, at which time Clark's experience beyond Ohio territory took a significant leap forward and for the first time brought him to the Illinois country.

Tensions between American officials and Spanish leadership in Louisiana country had increased as United States military actions against the British and Indians moved westward. Eyeing Americans suspiciously, Spain wanted to protect its trade and territorial interests along the Mississippi River. In spite of American assurances of peace, the Spanish fortified river installations in anticipation of an invasion. Nevertheless, official United States policy was to placate the Spanish and avoid conflict. American military leaders had their own suspicions about the Spanish, but doubted that nation's capability to fight England or America.

By an order dated September 10, 1795, General Wayne directed Lieutenant Clark to deliver a message to Spanish governor and military commander Don Manuel Gayoso de Lemos at his New Madrid headquarters, north and west of the present city of Memphis, Tennessee.[11] The message protested construction of a fort at the Chickasaw Bluffs, east of the river at the present site of Memphis, on American soil. Wayne also asked Clark to observe the military preparedness of the Spanish. In essence the general sent Clark to spy on the Spanish, as well as to deliver a letter condemning Spanish activities. Clark took one sergeant, one corporal and 15 privates with him, and headed down the Ohio River on September 15. Clark kept a journal of the trip, and wrote his findings in a report to Wayne.[12]

The boat journey down the Ohio took Clark into new territory and further west than he had been before. He brushed Illinois and saw a portion of the Ohio River that Lewis and he would travel eight years later. He first stepped on Illinois soil when the party stopped briefly at Fort Massac, and he recalled the stories of George Rogers' exploits 17 years before. The next day the soldiers camped near the site of Olmsted, Illinois. As his boat moved along the Ohio, Clark encountered other vessels and he learned about the Spanish from conversations with boatmen. He used every opportunity to learn of Spanish actions and intentions. He wrote of one encounter:

> I met a Boat bound from Illinoise to Post Vincennes, near the mouth of Cumberland River. I was informed by her crew that the Spanish Troops had taken possession of and were building a Fort at the Chickasaw Bluffs and that the Governor of the Natches was reported to be on his way up the river as far as new Madrid and intended to build a Fort and the Iron-banks, at or near the late Fort Jefferson, as soon as that at the Bluffs was finished.[13]

At the mouth of the Ohio, before turning southward, Clark spoke with the crew of a trading boat bound to Vincennes and learned that the fort being built at the cliffs neared two-thirds completion. On October 2, 1795, Clark's boat and party arrived at New Madrid, where Clark met Governor Gayoso, delivered the letter from Wayne, and asked for a reply to take back to the general. In conversation with the governor Clark tried to gain useful information about the fort and troops stationed there, but the official evaded questions.[14] Clark got a taste of the Spanish disdain for Americans that he encountered again in 1803.

In the reply to General Wayne, Gayoso acknowledged that the threat of invasion by the French from the American side of the Mississippi had subsided. Nevertheless, he sought to justify occupation of Chickasaw Bluffs based on information he had received that the United States would attack Spanish holdings to gain a strategic point overlooking the Mississippi. He also admitted building a fort and installing soldiers. He denied doing anything to disturb the friendship of Spain with the United States, or grabbing U.S. territory. Before leaving the next day on the return trip, Clark managed conversations with other boatmen and learned that the fort had 17 cannon mounted and about 370 soldiers in various capacities.

On the return journey Clark discovered what every boatman

and tradesman knew who battled the Mississippi River currents from New Orleans to St. Louis. It was no gentle boatride. Making good mileage per day was almost impossible. Clark wrote in the report of an experience that proved valuable to Lewis and Clark when they traveled against the Mississippi current in 1803:

> As I ascended the Mississippi I found its current Rappid
> and dificult and the Country on each side low, with no. of
> Islands. From twelve to fifteen miles pr. day was as much as
> I could conveniently make with the exertion of a good crew.[15]

On his way back Clark passed the remains of Fort Jefferson across from Illinois in Kentucky. In 1779-80 George Rogers Clark built the fort on high ground about five miles below the confluence of the Ohio and Mississippi to provide protection for proposed harbor facilities, and as part of development of an adjacent town called Clarksville. Two years later American officials abandoned the fort. Lewis and Clark stopped near this site on their way to the Illinois country.[16]

Weeks after Clark returned to Wayne's headquarters and filed his report officials granted Clark a furlough of undetermined length. He returned to Kentucky to help look after the deteriorating financial and legal affairs of George Rogers. In fact, all of the general's brothers did what they could to extricate him from lawsuits filed by Spanish citizens who claimed the general had confiscated their goods and supplies for his soldiers. One such suit pending in Vincennes court sought $24,000 in damages from Clark.[17]

William Clark resigned from the United States military on July 1, 1796. He had contemplated this move for more than a year and discussed with his older brother the need to pursue business opportunities, namely to manage the family land and farming operations. Clark's biographer summarized William's first phase of military and public service in the following statement:

> This initial period of his public life had given Clark much

valuable experience. He had learned how to handle and lead frontiersmen in a military capacity, and he had become thoroughly familiar with all the other problems and duties of a military officer on the frontier. He had gained a great deal of knowledge about Indians, their customs and traditions, and how to manage them. He had acquired useful experience as a diplomatic representative of his government, and he had met and worked with some of the leading military and political figures of that time and the near future. Not the least of these was Meriwether Lewis. . . . [18]

As part of the effort to clear the general's legal and financial record, William decided in August, 1797, to attend Vincennes judicial proceedings involving George Rogers' case. He left on horseback August 20, and started writing a journal that covered his exploits in Indiana Territory and the Illinois country through October 9, 1797.[19]

Clark most likely received specific directions and guidance from George Rogers, who had traveled the road—called "The Buffalo Trace"—from Clarksville to Vincennes many times. Clark arrived in Vincennes after an uneventful two-day trip. He remained there about nine days looking into the lawsuit and discussing the action against his brother. William concluded that he needed to learn more about the legal case from people in Kaskaskia, including John Rice Jones, a leading American lawyer and businessman in the Illinois country.

Jones, a soldier with George Rogers Clark in 1786, played a vital role in obtaining funds for the general's abortive attempt to fight Indian tribes in Northwest Territory. Without authorization of the U.S. government, Clark put an armed garrison in Vincennes and sent Jones to buy provisions in Illinois country. Jones went to Kaskaskia where Frenchmen and successful American traders remembered Clark's capture of the community and his benevolent governance.[20] Kaskaskians received Jones warmly, and guaranteed purchases of goods for Clark. The primary provider for George

Rogers was John Edgar, a prominent merchant who eventually became the wealthiest man in the Illinois country. A loyalist and officer in the American revolutionary cause, Edgar emigrated to the Illinois country and settled along the Mississippi River in 1784.

William wrote George Rogers of his plan to see Jones and Edgar. In a prompt response received by William before he left Vincennes, the general talked about the suit and expressed doubt that Jones and Edgar could help. But he urged William to make the trip into the Illinois country. "I find you are going on to the Illinois," George Rogers wrote. "I am pleased for two reasons. First, you may perhaps do some valuable business and also see a Cuntrey that it may hereafter be of an advantage to you to be acquainted with."[21] If he had only known.

Clark left Vincennes on horseback with two companions, identified only as "Mr. Porter" and William McIntosh, a native of Scotland and commercial trader in Vincennes who later became treasurer of Indiana Territory. They took a route to Kaskaskia that historians believe angled south of that taken by George Rogers and his troops from Kaskaskia to Vincennes to capture Fort Sackville.[22]

Clark made brief, but illuminating comments in his journal about what he saw in the Illinois country. On September 3, he wrote, "Pass plains to day more butifull then yesterday. Those plains are lareg & sufficiently rolling for Cultivation, some interspursion of butifull groves that give a handsom Variety to the view, others like an open Sea sorounded with a timber that appears almost of the reach of a days march."[23] William's experience contrasted sharply with his brother's winter excursion.

They reached Kaskaskia a day later and from the bluff overlooking the settlement Clark observed a deteriorated community. "I had a most pleasing view of a spacious plain in which stands the remains of that once flurishing Town, now nothing more then a heap of ruins, with stone walls falling in Chimneys standing without houses & roofs tumbling in."[24] He noted that Kaskaskia contained "about 100 houses & about 170 men."

Others traveling overland at approximately the same time made similar observations about the state of Kaskaskia. On his journey to the Illinois country in 1796, Dr. Hunter said of the community, "This village has been settled nearly as long as Philad[elphia] but now there are few of the Houses in any tollerable order. they consist of a few miserable remains of the former plain tho neat & useful mansions for the inhabitants . . . The French inhabitants not being pleased with the American Laws have chiefly gone over the missisipi to the Spaniards & sold their possessions here for a triffle. . . ."[25]

On this first trip to the heart of the Illinois country, Clark met some of the most influential and powerful citizens of the region. Those doors, opened by his brother George Rogers, never closed to William from that time on. He sampled the hospitality of gracious people, and talked with those deeply involved in public issues who set the tone for governance of Illinois. Given where Clark and Lewis would be in just six years, this otherwise brief sojourn to Illinois had immense implications.

Clark crossed the river to Ste. Genevieve, a few miles from Kaskaskia in what is now Missouri, then came back to the Illinois country by horseback and traveled north on the Mississippi flood plain to Prairie du Rocher and past the remains of Fort de Chartres. Clark stopped for the night at "Mr. Hulls Tavern," run by Nathaniel Hull who arrived from Massachusetts in 1780. He also spent a night there on the return trip. Hull became active in judicial affairs and fought Indians as a member of the local militia.[26]

Clark reached Cahokia on September 9, where he spent the night. His journal did not state with whom he stayed on this stop in Cahokia, but on the return trip he stayed overnight at the residence of Shadrach Bond, Sr., also known as "gentleman Bond," or his nephew Shadrach Bond, Jr. Both had farms in the region. The elder Bond had a long history of service with George Rogers Clark. His nephew, who arrived in the Illinois country in 1791, became the first governor of Illinois. The next day Clark took a ferry to St. Louis.

In St. Louis Clark made the rounds of the city's business leaders and social elite. At least one of his hosts, Charles Gratiot, had helped George Rogers during the revolution. Gratiot moved from Cahokia to St. Louis in 1781, where he married Victoire Chouteau, half-sister of Auguste Chouteau. In league with his in-laws, Gratiot became one of the region's most successful traders with the Indians, Spanish, and British throughout the Mississippi Valley. Most of the men William met and partied with were there when he returned with Lewis.

Clark paid his respects to Zenon Trudeau, lieutenant governor of Upper Louisiana from 1792 to 1799, and dined with the Spanish official. He stayed the night at the home of Gratiot after attending a ball given by Col. Auguste Chouteau, co-founder of St. Louis and fur trade pioneer. In his journal account of that night, Clark wrote, "In the evening went to a Ball given by Mr. Cl: Shoto where I saw all the fine girls & buckish Gentlemen."[27] Confirming that his guests rolled out the carpet for him, Clark wrote in the journal that he met the "gentlemen of character" in St. Louis.

Clark crossed back to the east side of the Mississippi where he conferred with respected men of the Illinois country. He stayed with "Mr. Bonds a rich farmer," most likely Bond Sr. While in Cahokia either on his way to St. Louis, or returning to Kaskaskia, Clark had opportunities to meet with other Cahokians. John Hay, a trader in the town and a political ally of Bond, became an important player in local government and politics, and a most intriguing individual in the history of Cahokia and Belleville. Nicholas Jarrot, another influential Cahokia resident, also may have met Clark. By 1797 Jarrot had become one of the territory's largest landowners and a prosperous trader with the Indians.

Clark returned to Kaskaskia on September 14, and picked up papers from John Rice Jones. He offered no details in his journal about the contents. Clark remained in Kaskaskia for more than two weeks due to illness. On September 23, he wrote of having dinner with "Col. [John] Edgar," and visiting with French settlers.[28] Distinguished French residents in the area included Pierre

Menard, a French Canadian active in the fur trade who later became the first lieutenant governor of Illinois, and Jean Baptiste Barbeau of Prairie du Rocher, a friend and political ally of Edgar.

The meeting with Edgar brought Clark in direct contact with arguably the most powerful man in Illinois country at that time, and a long-term player in business and political activities well past Illinois statehood. During this visit it is possible Clark would have been in the same community with William Morrison, who arrived in 1790. Morrison—referred to by historians as the "Merchant Prince"—became one of the best known businessmen in the Mississippi Valley. Lewis and Clark purchased goods from Morrison in 1803-04.

The horseback journey to Clark's home in Kentucky went quickly and without incident. On October 9, the journal ended with Clark at home. He reported to one of the brothers that he had succeeded in getting the lawsuit in Vincennes dismissed, and he had made progress in clarifying the status of George Rogers' land holdings.[29] At that time Clark had no idea of the importance of his social contacts along the way.

5.

The River Journey

Lewis and Clark wasted little time during their two weeks at Clarksville before heading down the Ohio River toward the Illinois country. Already well behind Lewis's original schedule for the journey due to delays in Pittsburgh, the pressure was on to get as far as possible before stopping for the winter. Regardless, every job, and every task had to be done carefully no matter how much time it took. Consequently, they worked as rapidly as care would allow.

Although there is no written record of what the captains accomplished at Clarksville, historians have pieced together an agenda from correspondence and later references. With two captains working now instead of one, they made substantial progress in planning the voyage during those two weeks, and setting priorities. The captains agreed on the first order of business: Enlisting members of the Corps of Discovery. From their earliest communication both captains expressed concern about finding capable and experienced frontiersmen for the trip. Lewis never intended to keep the crew members who accompanied him from Pittsburgh and they were dismissed.[1] This put pressure on the Clarksville stop to find solid prospects for the crew.

In a letter to Clark before they met at Clarksville, Lewis asked his co-captain to look for recruits who met specific standards for the expedition. Those included skills in hunting and outdoor life, and familiarity with hardships on the frontier. By the time Lewis arrived Clark had men lined up to be considered. Those who joined the party in October became known as the "Nine Young Men from Kentucky," and included some of the most familiar names from the voyage.[2]

In several cases Clark knew the young men firsthand. Most migrated to Kentucky and had been there some time. Private John Shields, the oldest man in the Corps, went to Tennessee in 1784. Born near Harrisonburg, Virginia, he had valuable skills as blacksmith, gunsmith and carpenter. Sergeant Nathaniel Hale Pryor, a cousin of Charles Floyd, journeyed with his parents to Kentucky in 1783. Clark praised the abilities of Floyd, born in Kentucky and the only member of the Corps who died on the voyage. The captains made Floyd sergeant from the beginning. Of this group Sergeant Pryor and Shields were among the few married men.

Others joining the ranks of the first full-time force of the expedition:

Private William E. Bratton, born in Virginia.

Private John Colter, born near Staunton, Virginia.

Private Joseph Field, and his brother, Private Reubin Field, both born in Virginia—their names often were written as Fields in journals.

Private George Gibson, born in Mercer County, Pennsylvania.

Private George Shannon, born in Pennsylvania, at 18, the youngest in the party.

Also joining the Corps in Clarksville was York, Clark's black slave and lifelong companion, bequeathed to him by his father, John.

If the captains had stopped with the men recruited in Kentucky the expedition force would have been about the size that Jefferson and other members of his administration expected. The working number for Jefferson was 12, in addition to the captains.[3] As the journals and correspondence reveal, Lewis never quite adopted that limitation. The party grew larger by twice the assumed number as the captains moved along the route to the Illinois country. The decision by Lewis and Clark to enlarge the crew had impact on total cost of the expedition, but that consideration may not have been upper most in their minds. The initial appropriation by Congress to cover all costs of the expedition, including wages, was $2,500, a rather handsome sum in 1800, but nowhere near the total cost of the expedition. Donald Jackson, using statements submitted to the government, estimated "total cost" at approximately $38,722.[4]

Lewis also took time at Clarksville to bring President Jefferson up to date on his activities in a letter dated October 3. Lewis included an idea of how the approaching winter might be spent after the party reached the Missouri River.

" . . . I have concluded to make a tour this winter on horseback of some hundred miles through the most interesting portion of the country adjoining my winter establishment; perhaps it may be up the Canceze [Kansas] River and towards Santafe, at all events it will bee on the South side of the Missouri. . . ."[5] He suggested that Clark might make a similar journey "through some other portion of the country. . . ."

The idea of such an excursion—leaving the full crew behind—landed with a thud in Washington, D.C. Jefferson made his opposition clear in a letter later in the fall, after Lewis had dropped his idea and the captains had decided to spend the winter in the Illinois country.[6] Delays along the route and political obstacles presented by Spanish officials in St. Louis already dissuaded Lewis from his scheme before Jefferson's response caught up with the party. After the letter from Jefferson, Lewis generally avoided "brainstorming" by letter with the president.

On October 26 the new crew, led by Lewis and Clark, began the journey down the Ohio in a keelboat and canoe-like boats called pirogues. Lewis, who kept the journal on this segment of the voyage, wrote nothing until they arrived at Fort Massac on November 11, the first point of Illinois soil touched by the expedition. They remained at the fort about two days before continuing. Although the journal entry by Lewis is brief, it provides material for speculation:

> Arived at Massac engaged George Drewyer in the public service as an Indian Interpretter, contracted to pay him 25 dollards pr. month for his services.— Mr. Swan Assistant Military agent at that place advanced him thirty dollars on account of his pay.—[7]

George Drouillard—"Drewyer" was the preferred version in the journals because Lewis and Clark never figured out the French spelling—probably was at the military fort on business, or was employed by the military there when the expedition arrived. He had lived a frontier life in Spanish-held Louisiana and Illinois country since migrating from Canada with his family.[8] He was the son of a French Canadian father and a Shawnee Indian mother, which gave him an understanding of frontier cultures. Lewis later convinced him to join the permanent party, although Drouillard remained a civilian employee rather than an enlisted man. Skills developed in the wilderness, specifically hunting and interpreting with Indians, made Drouillard one of the most valuable members of the Corps. After the expedition Drouillard returned to the region and engaged in the Missouri River fur trade with people who met Lewis and Clark during their stay in Illinois.

At this time Drouillard undertook a special mission. Lewis had hoped that as many as seven or eight army soldiers from Captain John Campbell's infantry company in Tennessee would be at Fort Massac ready to join the expedition.[9] None had showed up at Massac, and Lewis sent Drouillard to find them and join the main party later at Cahokia. Lewis did not officially hire Drouillard at that time, but agreed to pay him for services.

Clark knew his way around Massac. He wrote about the fort in his journal of the 1795 excursion to meet with the governor of Spanish territory. At that time Massac had a role in General Anthony Wayne's strategy against hostile Indian tribes and as an out-

post to take notice of Spanish military ventures. By 1803 the Indian threat had diminished, along with fears of military conflict
with the Spanish in Upper Louisiana.

Federal officials viewed the fort's tactical position on the Ohio
River, just above the confluence with the Mississippi and downstream from the mouth of the Tennessee River, as critical in protecting American interests in the Illinois country, beginning with
the French and including the British. The fort perched ideally 70
or so feet above the water, with unobstructed views of the opposite
shore and up and down the Ohio. For the most part, however,
military conflict passed it by. Only one minor battle was fought
near Fort Massac in its history.[10]

The history of the fort parallels the history of French and English occupation, international intrigues, wars with the Indians,
and finally the coming of Americans after the revolution. The earliest occupation of the Illinois country occurred under the French
flag that flew from 1673 until 1763. France initially laid claim to
the Mississippi River and its tributaries by virtue of exploration.
During that time the French settled outposts at Kaskaskia and
Cahokia, and developed a Mississippi Valley fur trade. Illinois and
the eastern part of the Mississippi came under control of England
at the conclusion of the French and Indian War, when the British
defeated the French in several major North American battles. France
ceded country west of the Mississippi to Spain. That occupation
lasted until after the American Revolution in 1776.

Coinciding with these events, the French built a fort at the
Massac site in 1757 to protect settlements and guard against invasion by the British and Indians. They named the installation Fort
Ascension because workers drove the first stakes on Feast Day of
the Ascension.[11] The French stationed about 100 soldiers there.
Sometime in 1759 or 1760 the French strengthened the installation and renamed it Fort Massiac for a French government official.
They operated the fort until 1764 then abandoned Massiac before
British troops arrived at the site in 1765. The British had similar
interests in protecting trade routes along the Ohio and Missis

sippi, and at one time considered building a fort closer to the mouth of the Ohio. However, the British neither built a new fort nor maintained the old, and allowed Massiac to deteriorate.[12] That was the state of Fort Massac—the American name—when George Rogers Clark and his frontier army appeared in 1778.

The United States refortified Massac in 1794 because of continuing threats from Indians and the British. When Clark visited in 1795 the garrison numbered about 40 men. By the end of that year, new commander Zebulon Pike had increased the count. He was the father of explorer Zebulon Montgomery Pike, for whom Pike's Peak in Colorado is named.[13] Pike remained at Massac until the U.S. temporarily abandoned the fort again in 1801, this time in favor of constructing Cantonment Wilkinsonville further down the Ohio on the Illinois side. President Jefferson closed that installation and reopened Massac in 1802 with Captain Daniel Bissell commanding. Bissell remained there until 1808.

Lewis and Clark concluded their business quickly at Massac, and left late in the afternoon of November 13 with two additional members of the crew. Captain Bissell had been expecting Lewis and Clark, having received a letter from Secretary of War Henry Dearborn urging cooperation in selecting soldiers for the trip. Dearborn also had communicated the same message to Bissell's brother, Russell, commander of an infantry company at Kaskaskia, and to Captain Amos Stoddard, commander of an artillery unit at Kaskaskia. Dearborn presented in the letter the desired characteristics for expedition recruits: " . . . sobriety, integrity, and other necessary qualifications. . . ."[14]

It is believed that John Newman and Joseph Whitehouse transferred to the Corps from Captain Bissell's company at Fort Massac.[15] Newman, born in Pennsylvania, became a discipline problem for the captains and they sent him back to St. Louis from the Mandan Indian villages on the Missouri River in 1805. Whitehouse, born in Virginia, also spent time in Kentucky before joining the captains. He kept a journal that has survived.

On the first day after leaving Fort Massac the party went about three miles and camped in what now is McCracken County, Kentucky. The following day the party passed the site of Cantonment Wilkinsonville, named for General James Wilkinson, in present-day Pulaski County, Illinois, and camped close to the confluence of the Ohio and Mississippi rivers, near the location of Cairo, Illinois. Boats and men remained in the vicinity of the two rivers camped on soil that is now part of Alexander County, Illinois, for as many as six days, while the party experimented with readings of latitude and longitude, and took day trips to nearby locations.[16]

A small group, including Lewis, crossed to Spanish soil on the western shore of the Mississippi on November 16. They encountered Delaware and Shawnee Indian camps and Lewis was offered three beaverskins for his dog Seaman. Lewis wrote, " . . . of course there was no bargan, I had given 20$ for this dogg myself."[17] The captains took instrument measurements on November 17, and remained at the Cairo site the next day.

On November 18, Lewis and Clark with eight men rowed a canoe to the opposite side of the Ohio where they visited the site of old Fort Jefferson. This had special meaning to Clark because his brother George Rogers chose the location, built a fort there and named it for Thomas Jefferson. It stood a few miles below present Wickliffe, Ballard County, Kentucky, just above Mayfield Creek. The exact campsites of the Corps for November 18 and 19 are unknown, although the party remained in the Cairo vicinity.

Lewis and Clark broke camp on November 20 and took the Ohio River to its confluence with the Mississippi. They are believed to have camped in Alexander County, Illinois, one more night. The following day they spent their first full day on the Mississippi, beginning the arduous upstream trip to the heart of the Illinois country: Kaskaskia, Cahokia, St. Louis, and their winter camping grounds on the Wood River in what is now Madison County.

From their first full day on the Mississippi, the co-captains and crew discovered the river gave up miles grudgingly. In the week of travel from the mouth of the Ohio to Kaskaskia the boats made anywhere from 10 to 13 miles a day, with everyone working steadily at the oars eight hours or more. In addition to the current and varying depths, the Mississippi was strewn with small islands that made it necessary to swerve, dodge and wind a course.[18]

Arlen J. Large, a student of the expedition, wrote that the Mississippi experience convinced the captains they needed a larger crew than previously considered for the upstream journey on the Missouri.[19] As learned earlier, William Clark experienced the difficulty of rowing against the current on his short trip to Louisiana in 1797, and it can be assumed that Lewis and Clark knew they needed a large party to negotiate the Missouri. Arlen Large said the exact number of the crew authorized by officials in Washington varied in correspondence and orders from the secretary of war. Lewis, on the other hand, always seemed to be thinking of ways to enlarge the crew in light of need.

At the end of that first day on the Mississippi, after traveling eleven miles, crew and captains camped on an island between Alexander County, Illinois, and the west shore. On November 22 Lewis mentioned passing two keelboats loaded with dry goods and whiskey for Kaskaskia. The crew kept rowing, and made a mile or two more than the day before. The party stopped the evening of November 23 at Cape Girardeau—now in Missouri— where Lewis went ashore to meet with Louis Lorimier, a controversial figure in early American history and a successful businessman in Spanish Louisiana. Due to illness Clark stayed with the crew.[20]

Born near Montreal, Lorimier fought with the British during the American Revolution and led raiding parties of Indians into Kentucky. He tangled on several occasions with the forces of George Rogers Clark. After the war, Lorimier accepted a land grant from Spain and moved to Upper Louisiana where he built a large trade with Indian tribes. In spite of his of anti-American activities, Lorimier became an Indian agent for the United States after the Louisiana Purchase.

Bygones were bygones that night in Cape Girardeau. Lorimier entertained Lewis at a lavish dinner and the captain wrote glow-

ingly of the party, the women in attendance and Lorimier's courtesies. Lewis returned to the boats that night. Lewis and Clark
resumed the voyage the next day, continuing up river mostly along
the western side, although they observed locations in Illinois. They
camped on a rocky bar near the Louisiana side that night.

For the first time since leaving the Ohio River, Lewis wrote
extensively about an Illinois location in his diary of November 25.
The object of interest was the mouth of the Big Muddy River. The
boats did not explore the Big Muddy, or stay long in observing its
waters, but Lewis wrote in some detail, in all likelihood from advance information about the river. Lewis said:

> It is navigable thirty or forty mils in high water; and heads in
> extensive plains with the Saline of the Ohio and the Little
> Wabash a branch of the Great Wabash—there are many
> fine mines of pitt Coal on this stream, and one not far from
> its mouth whence boats asscend in common and high tide
> are loaded with and transport it the Saline on W. of
> mississippi and to Kaskaskias & elsewhere for the use of the
> blacksmiths and other artizans. . . . [21]

The Big Muddy is one of only two major rivers in Illinois that
empties into the Mississippi below the Illinois River. The Big
Muddy drains an area of 140 miles in length and runs through
Jackson County in southern Illinois. The reference to coal beds by
Lewis underscores the importance of coal to the southern Illinois
economy even at this early stage in history.

That night, and for the next two days, the boats stayed close
to the western shore and camped at sites in the vicinity. On November 28, Lewis and Clark came to Kaskaskia, the first American
settlement of any size since they left Clark's home in Indiana Territory. The stop, which lasted until December 3, for Clark and the
crew, and until December 5, for Lewis, provided a respite from the
week's rowing upstream and an opportunity for the captains to
conduct important business.

6.

Adding to the Corps

Accounts of the arrival of Lewis and Clark in the Illinois country place emphasis on occurrences in Cahokia and St. Louis. Little time is spent on the first stop at Kaskaskia, in part because Lewis and Clark provided details of their meetings further up river, and they did not chronicle the Kaskaskia visit.

To place the Kaskaskia stopover in perspective, the focus must be on subsequent events and correspondence to help evaluate those five days. Primarily, the captains added several soldiers to their party, and began gathering information from informed Kaskaskia citizens about what stretched ahead on the Mississippi, and then up the Missouri. They took scientific readings, as they had done at the mouth of the Ohio, and replenished supplies and stocked up for the winter camp. They spent time with experienced merchants and traders, the first of the Illinoisans who contributed generously to the captains' education about the immediate region and beyond.

William Clark knew this territory. He must have looked around the community to see what changes had occurred since his visit in 1797. He no doubt located people with whom he had visited, including John Edgar, a powerful person in Randolph County where Kaskaskia was the county seat. The checklist would have contained the names of traders William Morrison and Pierre Menard, and John Rice Jones, his brother's supporter. Clark had an opportunity to again thank those who had cared for him during an illness on the previous visit.

For Lewis, this was new territory, although Clark surely told him about the Kaskaskians. Given his earlier visit, Clark could take responsibility for introducing Lewis to the leading citizens who anxiously awaited hearing of plans for the journey from President Jefferson's former secretary.

High on the priority list for Lewis and Clark would have been contacting commanding officers of army companies posted near the town. Captain Russell Bissell, brother of Captain Daniel Bissell at Fort Massac, commanded a company of the First Infantry at Kaskaskia, and Captain Amos Stoddard commanded an artillery company on temporary duty in the area. Bissell and Stoddard had received letters from Secretary of War Dearborn instructing them to cooperate with Lewis and Clark. Dearborn implored the commanders "to furnish one Sergeant & Eight good Men who understand rowing a boat to go with Capt. Lewis as far up the River as they can go & return with certainty before the Ice will obstruct the passage of the river."[1]

Stoddard and his company already had orders from Dearborn to establish an American military post at Cahokia upon completion of the Louisiana Purchase transaction, expected late in 1803. The secretary of war later canceled this plan and ordered the artillery company to remain at Kaskaskia. Stoddard, who assumed the role of military and civil leader in St. Louis after completion of the Louisiana land acquisition by the United States, surfaces repeatedly as a faithful associate of the captains.[2] Stoddard and Lewis established an especially close working relationship. Historian Ernest Staples Osgood writes:

> He was in close touch with Lewis and Clark during the whole Dubois [winter camp] period . . . There seems no doubt that the Virginian, the Kentuckian and the Connecticut Yankee [Stoddard] became strong friends. Before Lewis left, he designated Stoddard as his agent in St. Louis. . . .[3]

No wonder then, that Lewis, Clark and Stoddard, all with histories of military life and battles for the United States, found immediate comfort with each other. On the frontier, military service often became the closest personal bond among men. Born in Connecticut in 1762, Stoddard grew up in Massachusetts. In 1779 at age 17 he enlisted in the Continental Army and served until the end of the war, in such notable contests with the British as the Battle of Yorktown. In his memoirs Stoddard recalled a special moment at Yorktown: " . . . Who should appear but our beloved [General] Washington, who had just arrived and lost no time in viewing and receiving the salutations of the troops." After the war Stoddard interrupted his military career, became a lawyer and political figure in Massachusetts and rejoined the army as a captain of artillery in 1798. Stoddard saw combat again during the War of 1812 and died of wounds received fighting the British at Fort Meigs, Ohio, in 1813.[4]

The soldiers whom Lewis and Clark enlisted in Kentucky and at Fort Massac had opportunities to make the most of their stay in Kaskaskia. When not on duty they could spend time with the enlisted men of Stoddard's and Bissell's companies and absorb the flavor of their first lengthy stop in the Illinois country. Although a number of them had served in wilderness situations, they had no experiences further west than Kentucky and Tennessee. French ways probably seemed curious to young men from places such as New Hampshire, Connecticut, Virginia, Pennsylvania, and Maryland.

There is no precise record of those men whom Lewis and Clark selected from the companies of Stoddard and Bissell for the journey. In a letter to Jefferson dated December 19, Lewis began, "On my arrival at Kaskaskias, I made a selection of a sufficient number of men from the troops of that place to complete my party. . . ."[5] Arlen Large surmises that Lewis may have kept the statement vague because he had by then exceeded the number authorized by Secretary Dearborn and Jefferson.

Large believes the captains signed up more than a dozen men, some for the permanent party who made the trip to the Pacific, and others who formed an escort group of temporary hires.[6] These escorts, or "engages" as termed by Lewis and Clark, were highly skilled French boatman who helped the expedition fight currents of the Missouri River to Fort Mandan in what is now North Dakota. The temporary workers returned to St. Louis after the winter of 1804-05.

Eleven recruits from Kaskaskia, six from Bissell's company and five from Stoddard's, have been identified. However, it is not clear how many joined Lewis and Clark immediately in Kaskaskia, or later at winter camp.[7] Some became members of the permanent party, and a few returned after winter at the Mandan villages, with messages, artifacts and documents for President Jefferson. A few names are familiar from the Lewis and Clark journals and notes.

Patrick Gass, born in Pennsylvania, became a sergeant during the expedition after the death of Charles Floyd and wrote a widely published journal. He outlived everyone who made the journey.

Sergeant John Ordway, born in New Hampshire, next in command to the captains during winter camp on the Wood River, kept a journal.

Others who apparently signed up in Kaskaskia are:

Private John Boley, from Pennsylvania, a member of later expeditions with Zebulon Pike.

Private John Collins, from Maryland.

Private Peter M. Weiser, born in Pennsylvania.

Private Richard Windsor, home territory not known.

Private John Dame, born in New Hampshire.

Private John Robertson, New Hampshire.

Private Ebenezer Tuttle, born in Connecticut.

Private Issac White, from Massachusetts.

Private Alexander Hamilton Willard, New Hampshire.

After visiting Kaskaskia, Lewis and Clark had recruited about 25 crew members, including Drouillard and York, although not all were with Clark's party immediately after Kaskaskia. They added other members at winter camp and recruited temporary crew from

St. Louis during the winter. A group of eight recruits from Tennessee, four of whom remained, did not arrive until later in December. Lewis and Clark did not make a final decision on the permanent party until April and May, 1804, after observing their talents and behavior for several months. Even after assembling all the military records and journals, and with the diligent work of historians, there never has been a precise roster of the full company that traveled from the Illinois country to Fort Mandan.

7.

The Kaskaskians

Kaskaskians who entertained the captains and catered to their needs included a number of intriguing, wealthy and successful frontiersmen. Additionally, they had experiences of benefit to the captains. None ranked higher on that list than John Edgar, who brought to conversations with Lewis and Clark an array of experiences with U.S. military leaders, national officials and the Clark family.

Edgar took the Illinois country by storm in those early territorial days. Looking for business opportunities and anxious to speculate in land, he came to Kaskaskia in 1784 at about 50 years of age. During close to another half century in Illinois before he died, Edgar became the region's richest man and largest landowner in the territory, judge and jury of the frontier, the Lord of Kaskaskia. A politician of immense skill and agility with the nerve to battle anyone and any institution, Edgar, an Irishman, could be on any one or both sides of an issue, but never in the middle. Edgar cut a truly incredible swath on the frontier given the primitive nature of life and communications in Illinois country. By today's standards Edgar would be considered a tycoon and political force. Dynamic and commanding, he also was a bundle of contradictions.

Edgar helped average people, while alienating intellectuals and educated French settlers. He answered many calls in the name of loyalty and patriotism for the United States. At the same time he relentlessly pestered the government for personal subsidies, favors, reimbursements and land grants. Edgar's aggressive accumulation of land led to charges of forgery, perjury and fraud.[1] He had important friends, and sizable enemies, some of whom Lewis and Clark encountered before they left the Illinois country.

Accounts of Edgar's life before the time of his arrival in Kaskaskia depend mostly on statements he wrote, and word of mouth from others who witnessed events. As principal chronicler of his own life until 1784, Edgar left a dramatic story for those who were interested.[2]

A native of Belfast, Ireland—his year of birth is presumed to be 1733—Edgar migrated to Canada after a year in Albany, New York, where he worked as ship commander on Lakes Huron and Erie from 1772-1775.[3] Edgar entered the business world at that point, opening a retail trade store in Detroit. He accumulated a sizable fortune trading with Indians and the British.

At some point during those years he married Rachel Brown, also a native of Belfast who had lived a number of years in the Boston area. There is no record of the marriage, nor have details of their courtship survived. She had arrived in the colonies several years before, married an Englishman and bore him four children.[4] The husband and the four children died. When the American Revolution began, Edgar and his wife lived in Detroit, the heart of British strength in the Old Northwest.

If Rachel resembled the lavish descriptions of her, she caught everyone's eye. One writer said, "Above all, she was an incredibly beautiful woman. She was a tall, cornsilk blond with eyes a deep marine blue; she moved with an innate gracefulness so pronounced that nearly any man who saw her stopped dead in his tracks just to watch her pass."[5] Besides her stunning beauty, she liked wearing fine jewelry, furs and expensive lace. Friends never failed to mention her intelligence, flair for dancing and gift for conversation.[6] She died in 1822 at age 86. William Clark likely met Rachel in

1797 when he dined at the Edgar home, and again when Lewis and Clark arrived at Kaskaskia in 1803.

While living in Detroit John and Rachel developed strong sympathies for American revolutionaries. It is possible this patriotic fervor came initially from Rachel, who is believed to have spent time before their marriage in the household of Martha Washington, wife of George Washington. Rachel often showed visitors in Kaskaskia a keepsake watch given to her by Martha.[7] Together John and Rachel resolved to help Americans, even though surrounded by British partisans in an environment of intrigue and high risk. The Edgars plotted and schemed as full partners. There never has been any doubt that Rachel assumed a major role in events that unfolded.

As early as 1776 John used the Detroit retail trade store as a place to collect rumors, gossip and military intelligence that he provided in letters smuggled to George Rogers Clark in Ohio.[8] That was small play when compared to their next move. The couple plotted to help escaped American prisoners and British defectors make their way through Indian country to American lines. The precise number John and Rachel assisted is unknown but there is sufficient evidence they operated their own "underground railroad" for some time before luck ran out. Edgar wrote in an 1813 recollection about two specific instances when he helped escapees get out of Detroit.

The first episode occurred early in 1779. It involved the famous Indian fighter and frontiersman Simon Kenton, who had a military connection with George Rogers Clark and the capture of Kaskaskia and Fort Sackville at Vincennes. Indians captured Kenton as he roamed the Ohio frontier fighting for American interests, and turned him over to the British in Detroit.[9] His captors hoped Kenton would provide information about George Rogers Clark and American soldiers. To encourage cooperation, the British granted Kenton extraordinary freedom to move about as long as he remained in Detroit. In time Kenton found his way to Edgar's trading post and also made the acquaintance of Rachel. In May,

Kenton prepared to escape with two British prisoners. The Edgars became his co-conspirators. Interestingly, Kenton shared the escape plan first with Rachel, who later told John.[10]

One day soon after the plan became known, Kenton and Edgar were alone at the trading house. Without comment Edgar left Kenton and went to the loft where he gathered a large pile of moccasins. He returned to Kenton and dumped the moccasins on the counter, telling Kenton to take what he liked. Kenton said years later that he thought about the 400-mile journey ahead of him and selected two of the best he could find.[11] Neither man asked questions and no money changed hands. The Edgars provided guns, ammunition, and provisions for Kenton and two companions. Kenton successfully reached George Rogers Clark's army.[12]

There are numerous unconfirmed accounts of the Kenton escape and how Rachel helped. Kenton commented later to a friend: "It was on the [3] June, 1779. Mrs. Edgar had given me a rifle, a pouch of musket balls and a horn full of powder. When I got the gun I went back to the swamp to hide. The officers were shooting after dark and their servants [watching] their course, so I had to be very cautious."[13]

In a few weeks another opportunity arose to help seven Americans escape, and for letters to be sent from Edgar to George Rogers Clark. This time John and Rachel furnished arms, provisions and clothing for the escapees. The seven made it no further than a village of Miami Indians outside Detroit where they were captured and returned. Under pressure from British officials and apparently in an attempt to save their skins, two of the seven implicated Edgar.[14] British officials prepared charges against Edgar for helping Americans escape, and for providing intelligence to Americans about Indian tribes.[15]

On August 24, John Edgar rode a horse from Detroit to the couple's country home where he discovered British sentries and the commandant of Detroit waiting for him. They arrested Edgar, put him in irons and confined him aboard a ship headed to Fort Niagara.[16] The British seized his homes in Detroit and the countryside and confiscated goods at the retail store. Edgar wrote of deprivation and cruelty en route to Fort Niagara where he remained in prison about 18 months. At his next detention site in Montreal, Edgar received daily liberty as long as he appeared for muster each morning.

In Montreal, Edgar made the acquaintance of Thomas Johnston, an American under house arrest by the British in Montreal. Johnston knew of Edgar's hope to escape, and desire to carry information of importance to the American military. Johnston revealed to Edgar that British officials and residents of an area that later became the state of Vermont had entered a conspiracy to deliver the territory to Canada.[17] The surrender agreement included delivering a local militia force of about 3,000 soldiers, which then would be joined by 2,000 British troops. Edgar volunteered immediately to take the information to American officers in Massachusetts.

After pledging to Johnston that "nothing shall stop me but death," Edgar and a companion left Montreal at night and headed on foot across the Canadian border into Vermont territory, then across the White mountains of New Hampshire.[18] They dropped further south to Massachusetts along the Connecticut River. After discovering Edgar's escape, the British alerted Indian tribes and a military force known as Rogers' Raiders for the pursuit.

Hounded by the enemy in daylight, Edgar traveled at night, staying just out of the reach of his pursuers. At times he hid while Rogers' Raiders and Indians walked within a few feet. Edgar tramped through unfamiliar territory across streams and lakes, through swamps and tall woods. He went without food for more than six days, existing only on water before he discovered some wild grapes.[19]

Edgar contacted American troops on the Connecticut River in Massachusetts and they took him to Boston where Edgar gave information to Gov. John Hancock and Samuel Adams. Edgar wrote, "Gov. Hancock gave me dispatches to Genl Heath at West Point & which I delivered. General Heath gave me dispatches to Genl Washington at Philadelphia."[20] After meeting with Washington,

Edgar carried information back to West Point, to General George Clinton in Poughkeepsie, New York, and to officials in Albany. He returned from Albany to General Washington's headquarters.

Edgar received high praise from Washington and his military advisers, as well as members of the Continental Congress, for exposing the Vermont conspiracy. Edgar said later that the information "did in my judgement prevent the British from accomplishing the design [of taking Vermont]."[21] Historians doubt the timing of Edgar's intelligence, believing that U.S. officials knew of the conspiracy six months earlier. Regardless, Edgar's escape and long journey to the American lines gave him credentials for bravery that he used to his own benefit for many years.

According to Edgar, Congress then sent him to Connecticut to oversee the building of a ship. "I assisted in this work till the ship was launched, & I then returned to Philadelphia—During part of this time I had a commission from the president of congress, appointing me a captain in the navy."[22] On the basis of this account, Edgar sought grants from the U.S. government on several occasions to repay him for the property and goods he lost to the British as well as the ordeal he suffered in escaping from Montreal.

Edgar presented himself to United States officials after the war as a man financially, if not physically, broken by his experiences with the British.[23] Claiming to be a refugee from Canada, he pleaded for relief by Congress of losses suffered through his attachment to the American cause, and Congress complied. A special committee report to Congress said "that his suffering . . . requires the particular attention of Congress," and it was resolved that the Superintendent of Finance should give him "assistance . . . for his support" not exceeding one year, until he should secure employment.[24] On subsequent occasions Congress renewed the assistance. Edgar's critics alleged that he drew a navy captain's salary every year until his death.

The largess of Congress did not stop with pension payments. By act of Congress on February 18, 1801, Edgar received 2,240 acres of land. Law professor and author Francis S. Philbrick says the grant was the largest among the top five grants to veterans of the American Revolution.[25]

Looking for a place where he could put his money and business experience to good use, Edgar headed for Kaskaskia in 1784 to begin a life that he devoted to political activism and making money. He reportedly arrived with a stock of goods and money that enabled him to begin business beyond anything existing at the time in Illinois country.[26] Almost immediately he engaged in trade with Indians. He operated the largest flour mill in Illinois, and shipped great quantities of flour to New Orleans.

Those activities put him at the center of business in the Mississippi Valley, but his speculation in land turned out to be the engine that created astronomical riches. He began acquiring land from the French who panicked at the thought of living under American rule and headed for Spanish territory across the Mississippi. In their haste to leave, the French accepted Edgar's meager offers for the land.

At his peak, Edgar once held 49,200 acres in eight Illinois counties. Additionally, he owned large tracts of land in Ohio, Indiana and Missouri. Eventually the U.S. government validated most of his land claims, in spite of accusations that he obtained many by fraud. At one point federal land officials denied his claims to almost 100,000 acres in Randolph County, for reasons of forgery, perjury and inadequate proof of ownership.[27]

Opponents often doubted Edgar's honesty, but no one questioned his patriotism. From the earliest days in Kaskaskia he backed up stories of his Revolutionary War experiences with fresh examples of love for America. He came to the Illinois country believing strongly in the good works and judgment of George Rogers Clark, and in 1786 he got a chance to express that devotion in dollars. Upon request from a Clark emissary, Edgar guaranteed financial backing for a planned campaign against Indians along the Wabash River.

Edgar faced difficulties during the early years in Kaskaskia. It was challenge enough to live and work on the frontier, but Indians and unfriendly Spanish officials in Louisiana country tested the patience of Americans and the French. A crisis in the late 1780s brought Edgar and the U.S. government together again, under less than cordial circumstances.

After the revolution a succession of governing bodies in the eastern U.S. failed to provide services in the Illinois country. Clumsy efforts first by the Commonwealth of Virginia, then the early government of the U.S., left Kaskaskia and Cahokia without a governing structure or security from Indians. This exposed residents of Illinois to life-threatening dangers, and the preying of unfriendly Spanish officials across the Mississippi. The existence of Kaskaskia hung in the balance.

Watching with glee from Louisiana, Spanish officials offered land free of charges and taxes, and other lures to the French and Americans in Illinois. In many cases people accepted the Spanish handout. The Spanish made a bid for Edgar by offering him free land, no taxes and permission to work the lead mines and salt springs in Louisiana.[28] The Spanish then applied further pressure by shutting down trade on the Mississippi River and threatening to seize all American goods below the mouth of the Ohio River.

Meanwhile, the Indian situation became intolerable for Edgar and those remaining in Kaskaskia. Incited by the Spanish, Indians from the western shore of the Mississippi crossed to burn and murder, hoping residents would leave Illinois. On October 8, 1789, a band of Indians and a few whites attempted to carry off slaves belonging to Edgar. The attempt failed, but John and Rachel feared for their lives.[29]

Edgar and other Kaskaskians lost their patience. In frustration Edgar directed his attention to Major John Francis Hamtramck at the closest military installation in Vincennes. Impassioned correspondence from Kaskaskians to Hamtramck began on September 14 with a petition to the major signed by Edgar. This communication started a pattern by Edgar with military and civil officials of the United States on many issues that stretched well into the 1800s. Prolific and articulate, Edgar rarely let eastern-based offi-

cials go long without hearing from the Illinois country about issues of importance to the settlers.

In the petition Edgar referred to being outnumbered by hostile Indians, and the inability of citizens to conduct their daily
lives.

> The Indians are greatly more numerous than the white
> people, and are rather hostilely inclined: The name of an
> American among them is a disgrace, because we have no
> superior: our horses, horned cattle and corn are stole and
> destroyed without the power of making any effectual resis-
> tance; our houses are in ruin & decay; our lands are uncul-
> tivated. . . . [30]

He pleaded for a "commanding authority" to reverse the feel-
ing that citizens of the United States had been abandoned, then
ended the letter, endorsed as a "Petition from the people of
Kaskaskias," with a specific appeal:

> Thus situated our last resource is to you sir, hoping and
> praying that you will so far use your authority, to save an
> almost deserted country from destruction, as to order or
> procure the small number of twenty men with an officer to
> be stationed among us for our defonce; and that you will
> make an order for the establishment of a civil court to take
> place immediately. . . .

With ink barely dry on that communication, Edgar followed
with a personal proposition to Hamtramck dated October 3. He
promised to "furnish barracks and provisions for the said number
of troops, that is, flour, beef, pork, salt & rum, at the very low
prices that each of the above articles sell for in the country, untill
the arrival of the governor . . ."[31]

Hamtramck replied to Edgar and the citizens in a letter dated
October 14, acknowledging the plight of Kaskaskia and offering

temporary relief. He made no promise to provide soldiers and a commander.[32] Hamtramck offered good intentions but nothing tangible to relieve the suffering in Kaskaskia.

Edgar's lengthy reply to Hamtramck of October 28, escalated the conversation with more specifics and his own personal plight. He referred to the attempt by Indians to steal slaves, and his fear for the safety of Rachel and his friend John Rice Jones. "Every day we are threaten'd with being murdered & having our houses & village burnt. . . ." At that point Edgar drew a large and bold line in the sand of the American Bottom for Hamtramck and his superiors to see:

> The next spring it is impossible I can stand my ground, surrounded as we are by savage enemies. I have waited five years in hopes of a government, I shall still wait until March, as I may be able to withstand them in the winter season, but if no succour nor gouvernment should then arrive I shall be compelled to abandon the country, & I shall go to live to St. Louis.

He professed his love and loyalty for the United States and his desire to live in Illinois country, but if he stayed " . . . both my life & property will fall a sacrifice. . . ."[33]

Under the deadline imposed by Edgar, and at the urging of his military commanders, Territorial Governor Arthur St. Clair arrived in Illinois country on March 5, 1790.[34] It had taken him two years since being appointed governor to visit the far western edge of Northwest Territory. He proclaimed boundaries of the county of St. Clair, the mother of many future counties. He established judicial districts at Cahokia, Prairie du Rocher and Kaskaskia, the county seat, with courts of common pleas, general quarter sessions, and justices of the peace and probate. St. Clair provided Edgar and his friends with a lion's share of key judicial and administrative positions. Temporarily, at least, St. Clair responded to the requests of Kaskaskians, but only after extreme pressure from Edgar.

During his half century in Kaskaskia, Edgar lived in luxury and remained a central figure in the region. Befitting the First Citizen of Kaskaskia, Edgar built an impressive home in the community, a French style building one story high with dormer windows and porches. Over the years the grand structure served as a center of social and political activity. Lewis and Clark undoubtedly visited the mansion where the Edgars welcomed them.

After assessing Edgar's experiences there might be a temptation to portray Edgar as a frontier hero. That would be the conclusion that Edgar wanted, but it would be inadequate for a life that covered nearly a century of wild times on the frontier. He had heroic moments, just as he had other moments less heroic. For his time and place it is sufficient to cite Edgar as a unique, forceful human being who left a lasting mark wherever he worked and lived. Edgar died December 9, 1830.

Although a figure of importance in Illinois, Edgar shared the limelight with William Morrison, another American in Kaskaskia. In almost 50 years in Illinois, Morrison became the best known merchant in the Mississippi Valley. At the time of Lewis and Clark he conducted much of his business either at a store in Kaskaskia or one he opened in Cahokia.[35] The field notes of William Clark, written from the time of arrival at winter camp until the day the expedition departed for the Missouri River, contain several mentions of Morrison, enough to confirm that the captains did substantial business with him.

Morrison came to Kaskaskia in 1790 with a distinct purpose in mind: To make money. A 17-year-old native of Bucks County, Pennsylvania, Morrison and his uncle, Guy Bryan of Philadelphia, were partners in a mercantile business. Bryan tutored his nephew in the dry goods business, which he built into a respectable and successful enterprise in Philadelphia, and dispatched the youth westward. Arriving during the summer of 1790 with a load of merchandise and plenty of vigor, Morrison established the first store of Bryan and Morrison.[36]

Morrison built a large warehouse-store-office in Kaskaskia, which became the center of business. He dealt in trader and trapper supplies, dry goods, hardware, groceries, general merchandise, and Indian trade goods. Due initially to the connections through his uncle and a network of suppliers in the east, Morrison quickly extended operations south to New Orleans, north to Prairie du Chien, and eventually to such distant points as Santa Fe and the Rocky Mountains. John Reynolds, in his pioneer history of Illinois, said Morrison "was the first who laid the foundation of the commerce across the plains from the Mississippi Valley to New Mexico."[37]

Like Edgar, and maybe because of his guidance, Morrison dabbled in land speculation, accumulating several thousand acres. The exact number has always been difficult to pinpoint. Some accounts have him claiming 50,000 acres when Illinois became a state, with 20,000 being confirmed by the U.S. land office. Historian Robert Howard credited Morrison with 15,040. In 1814, federal land officials denied Morrison's claim to more than 27,000 acres in Randolph County, and accused him of fraud.[38]

Audacious and opportunistic are appropriate words for Morrison. There is one good example of his willingness to pursue business where others had been hesitant to go. By the 1790s, the Chouteau brothers in St. Louis, Pierre and Auguste, along with their brother-in-law Charles Gratiot, operated as a closed business society, preferring to do most of their trading through Canada. As changes in Canadian and Mississippi valley trade patterns began to impact the Chouteaus negatively, Morrison and Gratiot reached an agreement by which Morrison gained entry to the Chouteau clique and conducted substantial mercantile business. These opportunities left Morrison in an ideal spot after the Louisiana Purchase to extend trade operations to the Osage Indian tribe in western Missouri, and led to activity up the Missouri River and to the Rockies.[39]

Always on the look for business opportunities, Morrison joined with the early fur traders who followed the footsteps of Lewis and

Clark up the Missouri River. After the expedition returned to St. Louis in 1806, George Drouillard joined Morrison, Pierre Menard of Kaskaskia and Manuel Lisa of St. Louis in fur trade excursions to the Upper Missouri river country.[40] Furs brought back to Kaskaskia were sent to Bryan in Philadelphia for sale. At one time, Bryan and Morrison had 17 branch stores.

Of all the associations that bound Morrison to powerful men of the frontier, the one with Edgar created the most controversy. Morrison and Edgar held common beliefs on many issues, such as legalizing slavery, separating Illinois country from Indiana Territory, and controlling the local politics of Kaskaskia and Randolph County. As Morrison made his mark in business, Edgar placed his friend in the right political circles. Morrison held judicial positions in Randolph County from 1795 to shortly after 1800 when Indiana Territory, which included Illinois country, was formed. He never sought election to public office, but gained notoriety as a major part of the Edgar-Morrison political combine that did battle with Territorial Governor Harrison.[41]

While there is no mention of Clark having met Morrison on his journey to Kaskaskia in 1797, Morrison had been on the scene seven years by that time and had wide acceptance as a factor in business and politics along the Mississippi. Clark could not have spent many days there without encountering Morrison. When Lewis and Clark landed at Kaskaskia, Morrison probably was near the top of a short list of people to meet, especially when considering the needs of the expedition for provisions.

Lewis and Clark made the most of their time in Kaskaskia by adding substantially to the crew, gaining information about the Missouri River, purchasing provisions, and gathering information from well-traveled and experienced residents. Lewis also turned the boats and crew over to Clark, with this terse entry: "This morning left Capt Clark in charge of the Boat."[42] After five days docked at Kaskaskia, Clark and the crew headed toward Cahokia and St. Louis on December 3. Lewis left two days later and traveled overland for meetings in Cahokia and St. Louis.

8.

Getting Down to Business

Going separate ways for the first time since Clarksville, Lewis and Clark had distinct missions as their party moved north toward more heavily settled parts of the Illinois country. Lewis went by horseback to Cahokia and then to St. Louis for a high-level meeting with Spanish officials. Clark brought the boats, men and supplies upriver, closer to the location of their winter quarters. The captains planned to rendezvous near Cahokia a few days later.

In what now takes perhaps an hour to drive from Chester to Cahokia along State Route 3, the men and boats required four days on the river. Along this stretch of the Mississippi flood plain were the remains of early settlements in the Illinois country, many familiar to Clark. Here Americans had arrived not many years before in search of new freedoms, demonstrating a brashness and fearlessness uncommon among French settlers. They were the early representatives of a later wave of Americans inspired by the exploits of Lewis and Clark and lured to the vast territory of the Louisiana Purchase.

After spending the night of December 3 camped at an island in the Mississippi, Clark and the party pressed ahead the next day an estimated nineteen and a quarter miles, one of their most productive days of travel up the river. Toward the end of the day Clark and his party saw the ruins of historic Fort de Chartres at a distance of about two and a half miles.[1] Clark had seen the ruins up close in 1797.

Clark's party started before sunrise on December 5. Along the way, the captain noticed small American settlements, observing, "The Emigrent americains are Settled verry thick. . . ." Further upriver the party came to Fountain Creek on the Illinois side in today's Monroe County. About 12 miles up the creek, lined most of the way with settlers, was Bellefontaine, a storied community of early Americans.[2]

Clark stopped at the mouth of the creek where he met Daniel Blouin, a Kaskaskia merchant, who had promised to bring more provisions to the boats. The goods had not arrived, although Blouin said they were expected any minute. Clark and the crew went ahead a half mile from the creek and camped. They had traveled 37 miles from Kaskaskia in two days.

A few miles away from Bellefontaine on the Kaskaskia-Cahokia trail lived the Whiteside family at a place called Whiteside Station. They represent another epoch in early Illinois country history. The Whitesides and American settlers scattered throughout the Mississippi flood plain put the "America" brand on the countryside. Members of the family had frequent contact with Clark at winter headquarters of the expedition and they were among the first to settle areas north of Cahokia in present-day Madison County.

For 80 years or more the word "Whiteside" gave meaning to courage. First, family members stood in the armed force that shaped Illinois frontier battles against Indians in the early 1790s. Later Whiteside warriors left their marks on the War of 1812, Black Hawk War, Mexican War and Civil War. Furthermore, many Whitesides held appointive and elective offices before and after Illinois statehood.

Clark may have stopped at the Station or met some of the Whitesides on his visit in 1797. The family had spent time in Kentucky before settling in Illinois, and almost anyone who passed through that region talked with George Rogers Clark or his military associates. Such contact would have provided William Clark with advance information about the family and its exploits.

Original Whitesides lived first in Virginia, then migrated to North Carolina where many of the clan fought in the American Revolution. William Whiteside—often called "captain" because there were a number of family members named William—fought for the United States at the battle of King's Mountain, South Carolina, in 1780.[3]

William Whiteside and his brothers John and Thomas and sisters and their families migrated first to Kentucky in about 1788, and settled in Shelby County, east of Louisville. In 1790 three of William's brothers visited Illinois country and returned with a glowing report that convinced family members to leave Kentucky.[4]

Late in 1792 the family headed for Illinois, floating on flatboats down the Ohio to the Mississippi. The family armada—three brothers and family, plus a sister and family and the children of two other brothers—landed not far from present-day Fults, Illinois, in Monroe County on January 1, 1793. They discovered an abandoned blockhouse built 10 years earlier by Daniel and James Flannery about three miles southeast of present-day Columbia. The Whitesides refurbished the site and erected a protective fort.

By sheer numbers the Whitesides made an immediate impact on the American Bottom, but lasting impressions resulted from decades of frontier deeds driven by passion and determination. John Reynolds captures the essence of the Whiteside charisma in his pioneer history:

> The Whiteside family was of Irish descent, and inherited much of the Irish character. They were warm-hearted, impulsive and patriotic. Their friends were always right, and their foes always wrong, in their estimation. They were capable of entertaining strong and firm attachments, and friendships. If a Whiteside took you by the hand, you had his heart. He would shed his blood freely for his country, or for his friend.[5]

Stories about the Whitesides and Indians have been kept alive and retold countless times through the years by members of the family. The tales—some undoubtedly exaggerated—burnished Capt. William Whiteside's reputation as an Indian fighter, but they also illustrate how much survival in that region depended on being alert to dangers.

The exact number of settlers killed by Indians, or the precise number of Indians killed by defenders, will never be known. But American Bottom residents in the 1790s lived in fear for their safety. Making a life on the frontier had challenges enough—thick stands of timber, swamps, insects, malaria—without adding fear of capture or death by Indians. The ever-present danger forced many people to move further west or return to the east. The Whitesides made their mark on history because they stayed and fought.

Soon after the Whitesides arrived and rebuilt the Flannery outpost in 1793, one of their worst experiences with Indians occurred. About 45 Kickapoo Indians under Chief Pecon raided the outskirts of the settlement and stole a number of horses. Unwilling to let the Indians get away with brazen theft, William Whiteside recruited a handful of settlers to join his family in pursuit of Pecon.

Whiteside found the Indians camped near the present site of Belleville on Shoal creek. He split his small group in two and attacked the village. The Indians scattered, leaving behind guns, horses and belongings. In the melee, settlers killed the son of Chief Pecon, and the chief surrendered to Whiteside. Pecon quickly learned Whiteside had succeeded with only a few men, and a one-on-one fight between William and the chief ensued. Pecon escaped and rallied the Indians to pursue the settlers. Whiteside returned to the Station just ahead of the angry Indians.[6] Pecon got a measure of revenge a year later when his band murdered a young son of William's who had wandered from the fort to play, then shot and killed William's nephew near the fort. From that point William Whiteside had an insatiable desire for revenge.[7]

An opportunity to even the score with the Indians came a year later when Whiteside learned that a war party of Osage Indians had crossed the Mississippi River and camped on Canteen Creek in St. Clair County. Whiteside gathered a force of 14 men, including brothers, brothers-in-law and children, for an attack. The settlers surprised the Indians and killed all but one.

The Whitesides did more than fight Indians. They successfully settled and farmed, and participated in political activities. William served as justice of the peace and as judge of the court of common pleas in St. Clair County. Whiteside signatures appeared on petitions and documents urging territorial officials to separate the Illinois country from Northwest and Indiana territories. The Whiteside legend is secure in Illinois history by designation of Whiteside County, in the northwest portion of the state. State officials in the mid-1800s chose the county name not for any single family member or feat, but to commemorate the whole family.[8]

Clark's party had little time for observing the countryside as provisions from Kaskaskia arrived the morning of December 6. About 11 a.m. the crew pushed away from shore. Clark noted in his journal that Lewis had passed the mouth of Fountain Creek a day earlier on his way to St. Louis.[9] After making a little more than 10 miles the party camped for the night on the west side of the river, just above the current boundary between Jefferson and St. Louis counties. Rainy and chilly weather coupled with a north wind made the going difficult on the river.

Weather conditions remained blustery the following day. A north wind blew early in the day then changed to the southeast, blowing hard enough to take off one of the keelboat's masts. Clark docked at Cahokia Landing at 3 p.m., his journal showing this location as three fourths of a mile from the town of Cahokia and about two and a half miles from St. Louis.[10] Clark and his men stayed in Cahokia two days until Lewis returned from St. Louis to report on his meeting with Spanish officials. That was enough time for Clark to have contacted acquaintances, although nothing was reported in the journal.

Lewis left Kaskaskia on horseback, apparently by himself, and headed for Cahokia, spending two nights en route. Lewis caught a portion of the nasty weather that Clark encountered on the Mississippi, which would have made for an uncomfortable horseback ride. Lewis perhaps spent one of those nights at Nathaniel Hull's Tavern where Clark stayed on his way to Cahokia six years earlier. Lewis presumably followed the trail from Kaskaskia to Cahokia that took him past Whiteside Station and near the settlement at Bellefontaine, although no mention is made in his journals or correspondence.

Upon arriving in Cahokia, Lewis counseled with two people who others had recommended as interpreters and advisers for the meetings in St. Louis. They were Nicholas Jarrot and John Hay, both of whom played major roles in preparing the Corps for the expedition up the Missouri.[11] Hay deserves separate consideration because of his background, experiences, familiarity with the Mississippi Valley and the Northwest territory, and family history. This first encounter in December between Lewis and Hay quickly developed into a lasting friendship.

Lewis's only explanation for the choice of Hay and Jarrot as interpreters came in a letter to Jefferson. Lewis said he had "previous information" about the two, and had developed "every confidence" in their abilities to assist him. Lewis continued, "Both these Gentleman are well acquainted with the English & French Languages, a necessary qualification to enable them to be servicable on the present occasion as the Spanish Commandant cannot speak the English Language, and I am unfortunately equally ignorant of that of the French—these gentlemen readily consented to accompany me. . . ."[12]

Advance information about Hay and Jarrot may have come through Indiana Territory Governor Harrison who since 1801 had enlisted Hay as a political ally, and who corresponded with William Clark. As holder of several appointive positions in the Illinois country, Hay worked directly for Harrison, and the governor depended on Hay for information about the Illinois country and Upper Louisiana.

Lewis also could have heard about the two from former Territorial Governor Arthur St. Clair who knew of Hay's work until St. Clair ended contact with the Illinois Country in 1800. Hay's personal reach in all directions from the Mississippi, including territorial officials and maybe even Jefferson, meant his name would have been at the top of many lists for aid to the captains.

Jarrot had a region-wide reputation in land speculation and trade with Indians. It is entirely possible that Lewis and Clark heard about him in Kaskaskia, if not in Kentucky. Jarrot could have been recommended by Edgar, Morrison and Pierre Menard in Kaskaskia, where he traded for goods and knew the leading citizens. He was well known in the Prairie du Rocher vicinity after marrying the daughter of the leading French citizen, Jean Baptiste Barbeau.

After contacting Hay and Jarrot, Lewis's first priority was to meet with Spanish Governor Carlos Dehault Delassus in St. Louis. Lewis had not heard from Jefferson in several weeks and did not have a fresh report about progress toward an agreement with the French and Spanish for purchase of Louisiana. He knew it was in the works, but had no timetable. He was anxious to see if the Spanish had word, or would even mention the subject.

Lewis, Hay and Jarrot crossed the Mississippi River on December 8 from Cahokia and set foot in St. Louis. One could only imagine the anticipation Lewis must have felt in visiting the city about which he had heard so much. As the winter story of Lewis and Clark unfolds it features their contacts in St. Louis and the information gained from the intelligentsia. They spent much time there, and the people with whom they made contact proved useful. Soon he would encounter Auguste and his half-brother Jean Pierre Chouteau, and Charles Gratiot, the business people who put St. Louis on everyone's map. Having met these leaders in 1797, Clark had information to pass along to his co-captain on the history of the French in Illinois and St. Louis before the two parted at Kaskaskia.

As Lewis entered the community it must have appeared quite a contrast to more populated cities of the East. The largest community north of New Orleans and west of Louisville, and truly the jumping off point for everything west, St. Louis had just 1,000 inhabitants. Growth since its founding had been steady, but not extraordinary.[13] For all the trade that centered in St. Louis—the Spanish had given the founders of St. Louis exclusive trading rights on the Missouri—many of the most influential merchants of the region still lived and worked in Kaskaskia and Cahokia.

Although nearly 40 years old, St. Louis remained a small town with few roads and fewer amenities than towns in the eastern United States. A description of St. Louis in 1804 from the *Annals of St. Louis: Territorial Days,* provides a view of the community and access to the river:

> In 1804 the river front presented a perpendicular lime stone bluff, extending from the foot of what is now Poplar street, northwards to near Rocky Branch, over two miles, on a level with Main street, about forty feet above the ordinary state of water in the river. There was a narrow road on the sand at the foot of the bluff, used as tow path for cordelling boats, which, in high stages of water, was completely covered. The only road then and for some years thereafter to get from our present Main street to the river, was at our present Market street, which had been roughly quarried out by the early inhabitants to get to the river for water.[14]

While Lewis did not spend much time writing about the pleasantries of living in St. Louis, others who lived there at the same time offered glimpses. Beginning in January, 1804, until well past departure of the Corps of Discovery, Captain Stoddard lived in St. Louis as the first military and civil commander of Louisiana for the United States. An accomplished writer, he sent many letters to his mother and in 1812 published his recollections of St. Louis and Upper Louisiana. To Stoddard, the country was "beautiful beyond description." Stoddard told his mother in one letter, "The lands contain marrow and fatness, and produces all the conveniences and even many of the luxuries of life . . . A multitude of different berries and plums of delicious flavor" filled the countryside.[15]

He described St. Louis residents as more like townspeople than villagers. "The people are rich and hospitable, they live in a style equal to those in the large sea-port towns." He wrote of the social life of St. Louis, and the high cost of entertaining. Governor Delassus gave a dinner for Stoddard on his arrival and citizens honored him with another public dinner and ball. Stoddard felt the need to repay the courtesies, and he did, with a huge dinner that cost $622.75. The U.S. government refused to pay for the event, but he had no regrets "for the pleasure I have given and received is adequate to them."[16] Stoddard borrowed $400 from Pierre Chouteau to pay the bill.

Stoddard also described the housing in St. Louis, estimating "about one hundred and eight houses, and the best of them are built of stone. Some of them including the large gardens, and even squares, attached to them, are enclosed in high stone walls." He had described the homes of Pierre and Auguste Chouteau and Charles Gratiot. The town's most prominent house belonged to Auguste. The house was set in a block three hundred feet square between the public square on the river side and the church block to the west. St. Louis founder Laclede originally had constructed the building as an office and warehouse. Behind the house stood service buildings, slave cabins and stables.

Pierre Chouteau owned a stone dwelling, 75 feet across the front by 45 feet deep, to the north looking east over Main Street from its block of ground. The Gratiot house on Main Street, a smaller stone structure but grand nonetheless, faced east. These structures for the Chouteaus and Gratiot became familiar places for conversation and social events for Lewis, and occasionally for Clark during the winter and spring.[17]

Lewis had little time to drink in the pleasures of St. Louis that first day as his purpose was to meet with Carlos Dehault Delassus. Letters written later by Lewis to Jefferson and by Delassus to two superiors provide accounts of their meeting. Judging from the tone of each report, both men were on their best diplomatic behavior. Neither mentioned the presence of aides at their meeting other than Hay and Jarrot, although it would have been acceptable for Delassus to have an aide or deputy attending.

Lewis sought permission from the Spanish to take his party into Upper Louisiana in the spring. He told Delassus his plan to discover and observe in Upper Louisiana.[18] On this point Delassus doubted Lewis's sincerity that the trip was so innocent. Delassus wrote to his superiors, "I should inform Your Excellencies that according to advices, I believe that his mission has no other object than to discover the Pacific Ocean, following the Missouri, and to make intelligent observations, because he has the reputation of being a very well educated man and of many talents."[19]

Lewis's report to Jefferson of the meeting summarized the Spaniard's behavior as agreeable. Then Lewis added that Delassus "was sensible [to] the objects of the Government of the U. States as well as my own were no other than those stated in my Passports or such as had been expressed by miself; that these in their execution, would not be injurious to his royal master, the King of Spane, nor would they in his opinion provide in any manner detrimental to his Majesty's subjects. . . ."

Having extended all courtesies to Lewis, Delassus politely refused Missouri River access to the Americans. He wrote in his account of the meeting, "My orders did not permit me to consent to his passing to enter the Missouri River and that I was opposing it in the name of the King, my master."[20]

The announcement did not surprise Lewis. He assumed permission would be withheld until completion of the Louisiana Purchase. Delassus added that he would support an excursion in the spring, saying that by then he expected to have the approval of his superior. Lewis responded with thanks and observed in his letter "that it was not my intention at that time, to question either the policy or the right of the Spanish Government to prohibit my passage up the Missouri. . . ."

Concluding the conference on a festive note, Lewis spent the evening with the commandant—presumably Hay and Jarrot did too—and remained overnight. They left the next day for Cahokia and a meeting with Clark and the crew.

During the St. Louis discussions Delassus suggested that Lewis and Clark remain in the St. Louis area for the winter, perhaps in Cahokia. Apparently the decision for winter camp already had been made, as Lewis wrote Jefferson, " . . . I had selected for this purpose (provided it answered the description I had received of it), the mouth of a small river called Dubois on the E. side of the Mississippi opposite to the mouth of the Missouri."[21] Delassus reported the same information to his superior. Lewis made the decision during the two days with Jarrot and Hay, subject to final confirmation with Clark. It is likely the captains had talked about the need for a site in the Illinois country, anticipating the Spanish would refuse entry to the Missouri River.

The chosen location, which became known as Camp Dubois or Camp Wood, was on 400 acres owned by Jarrot in today's Wood River Township of Madison County.[22] Jarrot obviously knew the Wood River site contained timber for building shelters and had plentiful wild game for feeding the Corps. If Cahokia had been selected it would have meant a major financial payoff for St. Clair County and probably for Jarrot, but the party needed seclusion for its preparation, and quick access to the Missouri.

Illinoisans had varying motivations for making contact with Lewis and Clark during this time. Some people wanted to conduct business and make money, others felt honored to be in their company. There was a high curiosity factor, too, as indicated by the number of visitors to winter camp and St. Louis social events. The motivation for Jarrot to provide a campsite, and to assist Lewis in St. Louis, appears to have been nothing more than friendliness, and a desire to be associated in some manner with an intriguing project. He sold the captains a few goods—Clark's notes show a payment of $327.50 to Jarrot for pine boards used in a boat—but that hardly amounted to sudden wealth.[23] On a trading trip north on the Mississippi Jarrot made sure to stop at winter camp, and he provided information based on his contact with Indians.

Lewis, Hay and Jarrot returned to Cahokia on December 9 where they reported on events to Clark. The next day Lewis and Clark moved a short distance upstream to where East St. Louis is located today. Lewis returned to St. Louis to begin gathering information about the Missouri River, while Clark took the boats and men on toward the winter camp.[24]

Lewis reported on his St. Louis meetings and subsequent events in a letter to Jefferson almost a week after leaving Clark at East St. Louis. In it Lewis gave no indication of receiving any recent letters from Jefferson. Jefferson wrote Lewis from Washington on November 16 and in that letter addressed the issue of Lewis's planned excursion on the Missouri River during the winter. Lewis may have chosen to ignore Jefferson's letter, but more likely the letter was delayed by erratic mail service.

Jefferson told Lewis that he and others in Washington did not think much of the trip Lewis had proposed for the Missouri River. "One thing however we are decided in: that you must not undertake the winter excursion which you propose in yours of Oct. 3. Such an excursion will be more dangerous than the main expedition up the Missouri, & would, by an accident to you, hazard our main object, which, since the acquisition of Louisiana, interests every body in the highest degree." Then, Jefferson laid it on the line for Lewis: "The object of your mission is single, the direct water communication from sea to sea formed by the bed of the Missouri & perhaps the Oregon."[25]

9.

The Cahokians

In the days of Lewis and Clark it was impossible to spend time in Cahokia without recalling the historic days of that community dating back more than a century before the French fled to Upper Louisiana and before the rise of St. Louis. Today, the settlement's ranking position on the Mississippi is hard to imagine because Cahokia is almost lost in the urban sprawl from the eastern bluffs to the Mississippi.

Settled by priests from Canada, the community grew up around a mission and in the early days attracted an assortment of traders and drifters. Eventually families, mostly of French origin, were drawn to the area and created a stable settlement. Never able to take full advantage of its location on the Mississippi, and restrained by religious ownership of land and strict protocol, Cahokia in 1803 was in decline. Population had dwindled to about 700 people. Nearby St. Louis overshadowed the settlement in residential growth and business successes. Still Cahokia commanded respect in trade and commerce on the Mississippi. The town's residents included many men of wealth who lived on estates and in fine homes. Some of those who made the captains' stop in Illinois country productive called Cahokia home.

Little is known of the community's early history because a fire in 1783 destroyed church records, and civil documents from French rule have disappeared. Also historians have been unable to find any early diaries or journals, and few written reports by visitors or travelers exist.

Writing years later, John Reynolds provided a look back at French settlements along the Mississippi. His descriptions help in understanding Cahokia's days at the turn of the nineteenth century.

> The French houses were generally one story high, and made of wood. Some few were built of stone. There was not a brick house in the country for one hundred or more years from the first settlement. These houses were formed of large posts or timbers; the post being set three or four feet apart in many of them. In others the posts were closer together, and the intervals filled up with mortar made of common clay and cut straw. The mortar filled up the cracks, so that the wall was even and regular. Over the whole wall, outside and inside, it was generally white washed with fine white lime, so that these houses presented a clean, neat appearance. The other class of houses having the posts farther apart, the spaces were filled up with puncheons. The posts were guttered for the puncheons to fit in. These houses were used for stables, barns, &c., &c. . . . The covering of the houses, stables, &c., was generally of straw, or long grass cut in the prairie. These thatched roofs looked well, and lasted longer than shingles.[1]

Reynolds also described the French village layout for buildings and houses:

> The French villages were laid out by common consent on the same plan or system. The blocks were about three hundred feet square and each block contained four lots. The streets were rather narrow, but always at right angles. Lots in ancient times were enclosed by cedar posts or picketts planted about two feet in the ground and about five feet above. . . .
> A neat gate was generally made in the fence, opposite to the

door of the house, and the whole concern was generally
kept clean and neat; so that the residences had the air of
cleanliness and comfort.[2]

Some of the earliest comments and letters about Cahokia are
those written by Charles Gratiot, who spent four years in the community as a trader and businessman before moving to St. Louis in
1781. During more than four decades in the greater Illinois region, Gratiot conducted business from the frontier to the capitals
of the world with scoundrels, charlatans, braggarts, decent folks
and honorable businessmen. His travels took him throughout the
Mississippi Valley, Canada, the eastern U.S., and Europe. Through
it all, including brushes with bankruptcy and war, Gratiot had a
way of surviving and coming out on top. No matter where Gratiot
lived, he made himself available when people needed him. It fol-
lows, given his presence in St. Louis and familiarity with trade
routes, that Gratiot crossed the paths of Lewis and Clark frequently
in 1803-04 and became an integral part of mission planning.

Charles, the only son of David Gratiot and Marie Bernard,
French Huguenots (Protestants), was born in 1752, in Lausanne,
canton de Vand, Switzerland, where his parents' ancestors fled in
1665 to escape the purges of ruling French Catholics. Gratiot's
mother and father pushed Charles toward a life in the business
world at age 14, after the youngster received a basic education.[3]
Through the years he demonstrated the value of this early education in the creation of a large body of correspondence and well-
documented business journals.

Gratiot's parents sent him at that tender age to live and to
study law and bookkeeping in London with an uncle. At age 17
Gratiot joined another uncle, Bernard, in Montreal to learn the
fine points of fur trading. He learned well, for trading, especially
in furs, eventually made him wealthy. But the early years brought
him dangerously close to bankruptcy.

In 1775, after a successful trade trip for his uncle to
Michilimackinac—the center of fur trade activity in the northern

part of lower Michigan more commonly called Mackinac—he left Montreal for Cahokia to conduct business in the family name. There he discovered the facts of life in trading on the middle Mississippi River.

After his first major trading excursion, Gratiot wrote his father about traveling to Cahokia as a clerk with three canoes of merchandise to trade for furs with Indians and the French. "Trade there is done mostly by contraband, the two shores, Spanish and English sides, being near together separated only by the Mississippi river."[4] In other words, to succeed he had to smuggle the goods back and forth. Gratiot stayed almost a year longer than planned in an effort to regain the money lost when Spanish officials caught him red-handed and seized his furs.

During his first exposure to the Illinois country, Gratiot liked what he saw. Gratiot wrote his father about the Illinois countryside in the years between 1774 and 1776—before he moved there permanently—revealing an eye for the environment and culture, and for beauty.

> That country abounds in wheat and all other provisions, the swamps and rivers are covered with game, Swans, Bustards, Cranes, Geese, Ducks and of all varieties, which added to the heat, makes the people very lazy, and having besides in the immense prairies number of Deer and Buffaloes enormous in size, they hunt these with horses that are trained to this chace, the most of the Canadians that go to this country remain there . . .[5]

An observant young man, Gratiot also had a comment about the young women. In the same letter, he wrote, "The females are pretty enough although a little tawny, and dress in the French fashion, generally coquetish, aspiring after pleasure, amusing themselves, and dance much in spite of the summers' heat."

Gratiot's work with his uncle collapsed in disagreement over the sale of furs, and ended unhappily in a lawsuit. He wrote his father in disgust, "I found him at all times inexorable, and each time I supplicated him, he appeared to have as much pity as if I had spoken to a Bronze-Statue."[6] Gratiot formed a partnership in Montreal with John Kay, David McCrae and Pierre Barthe and headed to Cahokia in 1777 to open a store. Gratiot sought a business opportunity where he could operate on his own, and he also escaped the politics and turmoil of the American Revolution in Canada and the eastern U.S.

Gratiot had another reason for returning to the Illinois country. On the earlier excursion he spent time in St. Louis where he met Pierre and Auguste Chouteau, and the town's founder, Pierre LaClede. Equally significant in terms of his future, he met a pretty 10-year-old girl, Victoire, a sister of the Chouteaus. Upon his return Charles found an older and more mature Victoire, now 14.

With the Cahokia store, and one opened by his partners in Kaskaskia, Gratiot plunged into business with local citizens. They found him something of a curiosity—a French protestant—but by all accounts he charmed them and made friends easily. The stores sold utilitarian goods: Cotton, flannel, hats, pencils, buttons, pots, razors, gloves, and luxury items such as gold and silver lace, Irish linen and pewter goblets.

True to the tale of his life, nothing remained the same for long. Just seven months after Gratiot arrived, George Rogers Clark captured Kaskaskia and shortly thereafter seized Cahokia. Gratiot's first adventure with the Clark family began, as the Frenchman provided provisions for Clark's troops. Gratiot and Clark enjoyed a close association and encountered each other several times during the Revolution and after. In 1780, when Indian tribes and British soldiers threatened to invade Cahokia and St. Louis, Cahokia citizens asked Gratiot to write Clark for protection. Gratiot pleaded with George Rogers, "We are on the eve of being attacked in our village by considerable parties of savages and will not be able to work at the cultivation of our fields, if we do not have prompt succor."[7] The invaders were thwarted, with help from Clark.

Meanwhile, Gratiot's business fortunes sagged. The revolution limited trading activity in Canada and England, and Spain's restrictions on the Mississippi became onerous. During the anxious days of 1780 when war threatened near Cahokia, Gratiot moved valuable goods to St. Louis for safety. A year later he left Cahokia.

Gratiot's time as a resident of Cahokia ended in 1781 when he moved to St. Louis and became a Spanish subject. He married Victoire, then 18, and joined the wealthy and powerful Chouteau family.[8] He traded with Spanish approval up and down the Mississippi, and particularly in New Orleans, all of which were off-limits to Americans. The Spanish rewarded his change of residence with a land grant of 8,000 acres west of St. Louis, a part of which today is included in Forest Park, in St. Louis.[9]

He put behind him the frustrations of doing business in the Illinois country during the war years, and another unhappy partnership. With contacts around the world, and especially in the eastern United States and London, Gratiot attempted to open a far-reaching fur trade business with agents in England. Writing of this venture, which failed, Theophile Papin Jr., of St. Louis whose father Joseph Marie was a contemporary of Gratiot, said, "Had their (the agents) judgment equalled his indomitable energy and stability, he would undoubtedly have created one of the great fur trading companies of the world."[10]

Gratiot ingratiated himself to Lewis and Clark. He knew the coming of Americans west of the Mississippi River would open fresh business opportunities, and he wanted to be first in line. He procured goods for the Corps of Discovery, visited the winter camp, renewed his acquaintance with William Clark, and entertained both captains in style in St. Louis. It worked. Before leaving St. Louis Lewis named Amos Stoddard his agent for any transactions of the Corps and designated the captain to handle items sent back from the Mandan Indian villages. In his letter to Stoddard, he said that if the captain could not perform the duties for any reason, Gratiot was to take charge.[11]

The gesture of trust by Lewis was confirmed by a later assessment of Gratiot's character by John Reynolds. He said of Gratiot: "He was frank, open and candid, in all his transactions. . . . moral and exemplary in his deportment; and although he was never a member of any church, yet his conduct was approved by the wise and good of all denominations."[12]

On separate occasions Gratiot corresponded with Thomas Jefferson, Patrick Henry, James Madison, John Jacob Astor and other colonial officials and businessmen about a variety of subjects, including Louisiana Territory. He embraced the U.S. presence in Louisiana after Lewis and Clark, and became an enthusiastic promoter of American interests. Gratiot played a major role in the transfer of French Upper Louisiana to the Americans in 1804. Indiana Territory Governor Harrison appointed him judge of the First Court of Quarter Sessions (this court handled criminal cases) in 1805 while Lewis and Clark were on their way to the Pacific. He served as justice of the peace from 1811 to 1813, and died of paralysis on April 20, 1817, at the age of 65.[13]

Like many of the individuals who Lewis and Clark encountered—Hay, Morrison, the Whitesides—Nicholas Jarrot arrived in the Illinois country during the 1790s. He escaped political conflict in his birthplace of Vesoul, France, and came to America for the same reasons as others: opportunity and freedom. Arriving in Baltimore without contacts, friends or money, he stayed briefly, then went to New Orleans. He made his way north on the Mississippi River in 1794.[14]

A man of good breeding and education, Jarrot also was single, handsome and dashing. Reynolds said of Jarrot, "His mind was strong, active and sprightly."[15] Young French women along the Mississippi River must have found him attractive. Before landing in Cahokia, he stopped at various French settlements including Ste. Genevieve on the Spanish side, and Prairie du Rocher, just north of Kaskaskia. At the latter location he met the woman who became his wife.

Jarrot found his way to Cahokia where he opened a retail store to serve local citizens and looked for ways to begin trading with Indians. Almost immediately he began acquiring property in the Illinois country, perhaps with financial help from his father-in-law. Early in his stay Jarrot met and married Marie Barbeau, a young Frenchwoman from Prairie du Rocher. The marriage brought Jarrot into one of the prominent families of the region. Marie's father, Jean Baptiste Barbeau, owned large acreages of land and served as a local judge during the French and British occupations. Jarrot bought his first property in 1795 or 1796, and once he started there seemed to be no end. By 1815 he had title confirmed by Illinois territorial officials to 25,000 acres of land, mostly in St. Clair and Madison counties.[16] Determining the precise acreage he owned is difficult because of poor records and frequent transactions and trades for land.

His first wife died after only a few years of marriage, leaving Jarrot and one daughter. Soon thereafter Jarrot married Julia Beauvias of Ste. Genevieve, daughter of wealthy French parents. Jarrot and his second wife had six children, a number of whom became well-known citizens of Illinois. The Jarrots made their first home in a small building in the village, but they had their eyes set on something grander.

With a productive Mississippi River trade and growing real estate holdings, Nicholas and Julia in 1799 began construction of a magnificent house in Cahokia that stands to this day.[17] Jarrot House, completed a decade later, surpassed anything in Cahokia and St. Louis in grandeur. Materials used for construction came from the region, with one exception: Jarrot imported glass windowpanes from France. The architectural style compared to Maryland of that time, featuring red brick, and a white formal porch supported by Corinthian columns. The central hall and stairway, the Flemish bond front, and woodwork, were Anglo-American in character.[18]

Every room in the mansion saw heavy use. At one time Jarrot offered the ballroom on the second floor as the first school in Cahokia. The Jarrots entertained in the finest fashion, making the mansion a central place for dancing and balls. The gaming sessions at the house are among Cahokia's longest standing legends. Jarrot, witnesses reported, played the role of banker during the gambling, and when necessary went to his chest of money upstairs to keep a player in the game.[19] Mrs. Jarrot lived in the house until her death in 1870. It is an Illinois landmark today in Cahokia—without the Corinthian columns.

Jarrot conducted most of his trade with Indians on the upper Mississippi, at Prairie du Chien and at the Falls of St. Anthony, now Minneapolis, Minnesota. With this background as a successful trader with Indians, Jarrot had information of value to Lewis and Clark about the tribes and the dangers facing the explorers. His experiences on the Mississippi illustrated the need for caution.

Five hundred miles above the mouth of the Missouri at the junction of the Wisconsin River and the Mississippi, Prairie du Chien became a convenient meeting place for the Indians and traders.[20] British fur traders used the location as a jumping off place to encroach on Spanish territory west of the Mississippi. From Prairie du Chien traders ascended the Mississippi and Minnesota rivers, and headed west to the Red River, then north to Assiniboine River country and Lake Winnipeg. When Jarrot took goods to Prairie du Chien he conducted business at a major crossroads on the trade highway of the time.

Jarrot made at least annual trips to Prairie du Chien with goods grown and made in the Illinois country, and traded with Indians for furs. No matter how many times Jarrot made the trip, dealing with Indians presented high risks. Stories of fear, death and bravery—including those involving Jarrot—give testimony to the dangers. John Reynolds, in his pioneer history, recounts an episode that speaks to the dangers of trading with the Indians, and the importance of having a spotless reputation among the tribes.[21] The story begins with Jarrot and two men taking trade goods out from Prairie du Chien to a large Indian camp nearby. They anticipated no troubles.

Reynolds writes: "The Indians. . . . were frantic with rage

against him, because he was an American. This was effected by the
British traders. The Indians were determined to kill him, and take
his merchandise. Jarrot and his men were only armed with shotguns, expecting no enmity from the Indians. The warriors, to a
considerable number, armed themselves for murder and proceeded
out to the camps to meet Jarrot. The Indians raised the war hoop
and brandished their spears and tomahawks in the air. It was approaching an alarming crisis. Jarrot and men seemed doomed to
destruction."

At that moment one of Jarrot's Indian friends from the
Winnebago tribe confronted the crowd of warriors and let out a
loud cry used by Indians in battle. His action stopped the trouble-
makers in their tracks. Reynolds added: "The warriors saw the
danger they were in. One or more of them must be slain by the
friend of Jarrot if they persisted in the attempt to murder him and
party. The bravery of the Winnebago made them reflect, and they
desisted from the cowardly act, to assassinate the trader." The
Indian's heroic stand saved Jarrot and his associates. To cap the
story, Reynolds reported that the Winnebago Indian changed his
name to Jarrot. Reynolds said he met the Indian in Galena, Illinois, in 1829.[22]

Jarrot's land holdings became sources of success and trial. Much
of the land owned by Jarrot stretched north of Cahokia into what
is now Madison County. While St. Clair, Monroe and Randolph
counties constituted the cradle of white civilization along the
American Bottom, Madison County remained isolated and unsettled. Few settlers appeared in Madison County before 1800.
Being a shrewd land speculator, Jarrot sensed that part of the region would be the next to attract Americans.[23]

As one of the region's largest landowners, Jarrot found himself
caught up in land office investigations during the period of Illinois
Territory. One report of Kaskaskia land claims, revealed the office
had disapproved claims totaling 9,000 acres for inadequate proof
of ownership. While the land office accused other speculators of
forgery and perjury, Jarrot avoided such charges.[24]

Some of Jarrot's holdings in what is now Madison County had historical significance. A portion of the American Bottom near Cahokia, and just over the boundary in Madison County, is a rich archaeological site, dating back to unrecorded history where the earliest Indian tribes built mounds.[25] Jarrot's land holdings included the historic Cahokia Mounds. In 1808, Trappist monks sought a location for their mission in the Cahokia area. They approached Jarrot and he gave 400 acres for the monks to build a monastery on top of the highest mound that rises at the point where Canteen Creek joins Cahokia Creek. Now called Monk's Mound, it was known then as the "Great Nobb." The mission failed in 1813, but Jarrot's generosity toward the monks has remained a part of his legacy.[26]

In 1826, three years after Jarrot's death, his widow asked the state auditor's office in Vandalia for a statement of land owned by Jarrot. Although this may have been only a fraction of his real estate holdings, the totals are impressive. Jarrot's heirs owned 5,300 acres in St. Clair County, 3,680 in Madison County and 100 acres in Randolph County.[27]

William Clark gravesite and monument overlooks the
Mississippi River at Bellefontaine Cemetery, St. Louis.
Photo by Mary C. Hartley.

Likeness of William Clark anchors the memorial. Mary C. Hartley.

Replica of Fort Massac near the original site, overlooking
the Ohio River. Mary C. Hartley.

Memorial to George Rogers Clark at Fort Massac site
commemorates capture of the Illinois country in 1778.
Mary C. Hartley.

General George Rogers Clark. Courtesy of the Illinois
State Historical Library.

William Henry Harrison, governor of Indiana Territory,
war hero, and president of the United States. Courtesy of
the Illinois State Historical Library.

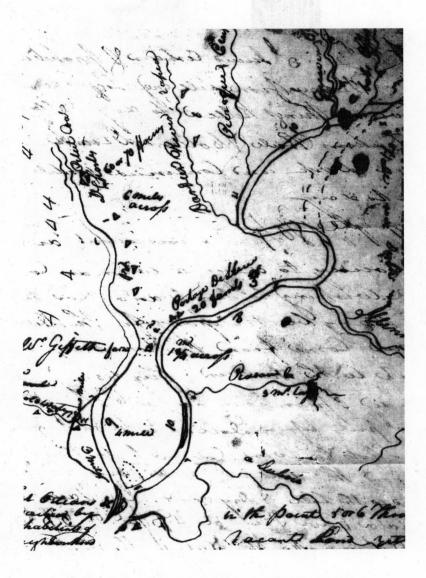

Confluence of Mississippi and Missouri rivers, drawn by
William Clark, 1804. Courtesy Yale Collection of Western
Americana, Beinecke Books and Manuscripts Library.

Grave marker of William Morrison, among those moved
from Kaskaskia village to Garrison Hill Cemetery near the
site of old Fort Kaskaskia. Mary C. Hartley.

John and Rachel Edgar's French-style home at Kaskaskia.
Courtesy of the Illinois State Historical Library.

General John Edgar. Courtesy of the Illinois State
Historical Library.

Pierre Menard's home near old Fort Kaskaskia site, built about 1800. Mary C. Hartley.

Pierre Menard, fur trader and first lieutenant governor of Illinois. Courtesy of the Illinois State Historical Library.

Monument and gravesite of Shadrach Bond, Jr., first
governor of Illinois, at Chester. Mary C. Hartley.

Church of the Holy Family in Cahokia, built of logs in
1799 and restored. The Parish is more than 300 years old.
Mary C. Hartley.

Nicholas Jarrot's mansion, restored and maintained at
Cahokia. Mary C. Hartley.

Charles Gratiot, friend of George Rogers and William Clark. Courtesy of the Illinois State Historical Library.

Auguste Chouteau, a founder of St. Louis. Courtesy of the Illinois State Historical Library.

The Lewis and Clark Historic Site in Illinois features a
replica of the keelboat. Courtesy of Brad Wynn.

10.

The Indispensable Man

Lewis and Clark met and conferred with successful and intriguing people in the Illinois country while they prepared for the journey up the Missouri River. Among many special individuals, John Hay of Cahokia ranked highly as a trusted helpmate and close confidant of the captains.[1]

This was no fluke. Quiet, modest, efficient, precise, and a respected family man, Hay had earned a place in the hierarchy of the region after less than a decade in Cahokia. Today he would be called an operative, wired to all the important people in the Mississippi Valley, and considered the steady hand of local government. Hay worked effectively behind the scenes, and had a reputation for giving sound advice. Lewis and Clark needed someone of his stature and dependability.[2]

The captains had their choice of the region's best. Why Hay? How did Hay become one of William Henry Harrison's chosen few in the Illinois country? How did someone who owned little more than a house on a lot end up equally powerful or moreso than land barons John Edgar, William Morrison and Nicholas Jarrot? Where did he get the information that seemed so important to Lewis and Clark? Why did Lewis and Clark trust him, value his advice, and give him access?

No individual in the Illinois country is mentioned more than

Hay in the captains' field notes and letters from December 1803, to May 1804.[3] Hay helped Lewis in St. Louis and Clark at Camp Dubois. He translated documents and interpreted maps. He passed on insights from direct experiences with Indians. He did all this while performing duties as chief administrator of local government in St. Clair County.

More than any of the people Lewis and Clark met, Hay worked effectively at all levels of society. For many he *was* local government. In such a position he knew people throughout the region. He approved business dealings, signed papers, witnessed wills, advised on law and procedures, and vouched for loans.[4] Without a huge government bureaucracy on which to lean for reassurance, the public looked to Hay for signs that government could work for them.

Hay and those who held public office faced daunting challenges. The frontier begged for order and precision, but government failed the efficiency test on many fronts. The land system invited fraud and needed reform. Residents spoke in a jumble of confusing tongues. The "frontier spirit" often meant taking action outside the law, or not recognizing that a law existed. Hay applied his skills and experience to provide a center of stability in a chaotic environment.

His view of life along the Mississippi extended well beyond government activities or citizen needs. Based on previous experience as a trader, Hay understood the method of exchange, how riches were made and lost, and the dangers of conducting business in the wilderness. He knew the barter system ("Bring me pelts, I will give you wheat"), and the people who made it work: Indians, British, French, merchants, and traders in New Orleans or Canada. Hay knew them by name and by dealings, from Montreal to Mackinac, Prairie du Chien to the Assiniboine, St. Louis to New Orleans, up the Missouri, along the Wabash, down the Ohio, and the length of the Mississippi. He worked in all seasons and under all circumstances. The day Lewis met Hay in Cahokia turned out to be a great day for the expedition.

Hay's contribution to the expedition of Lewis and Clark can

be appreciated by connecting him with the lives of others more notorious and successful. This includes his father's involvement with Indians of the Ohio valley and with the Clark family, Hay's trade business venture with Andrew Todd, his knowledge of Missouri River explorations before Lewis and Clark, and his political association with William Henry Harrison. These formed the base of knowledge that Hay shared with the captains.

John's father, Jehu Hay, played a major role in the military and administrative history of Detroit, Canada and the British Empire for 23 years from 1762 to 1785. But this broad experience did not assure him of respect by his countrymen or his enemies. In fact, history has not been kind to Jehu.[5] He had a significant role in one of England's most embarrassing defeats during the American Revolution, and that reputation dogged him ever after. On his personal journey Jehu accumulated more enemies than friends, including soldiers in the ranks as well as high government officials. All of these life-moments had impact on his son, John.

In many respects the life of Jehu Hay was typical of military men who lived and fought on the frontier and survived to fight again. He married a woman in her teens, fathered several children, and spent long periods of time away from home. Personal associations with British partisans shaped Jehu's fate. The relationship with Henry Hamilton, governor of Detroit and warrior against American interests, influenced Jehu more than any other. Hamilton is best known in American Revolution history as the "hair buyer," for paying Indians to scalp American settlers and bring the scalps to him.[6]

Of Jehu Hay's early life only the location of his birth in Chester, Pennsylvania, is known. In 1758 he entered the British army as an ensign in the 60th American Regiment.[7] Judging from that date, assuming he was 20 years old at the time, Hay might have been born about 1738. John Reynolds says in his pioneer history that Hay's wife was 10 years younger and was born in 1748.[8] Jehu received early military training at the British stronghold of Fort

Niagara, and achieved the rank of lieutenant in 1762. He first reached Detroit later that year as part of an army unit commanded by Major Henry Gladwin. The rest of his life would be entwined with that location and the military.

In short order Hay became embroiled in one of Detroit's memorable encounters with warring Indians. Chief Pontiac of the Ottawas led a large confederation of tribes in an effort to defeat the British and stop their westward movement. In the summer of 1763, after capturing several British forts, Pontiac attempted to bring Detroit to its knees in what is known as the Siege of Detroit.[9] Major Gladwin had about 100 soldiers to defend the fort against thousands of Indians. Those inside included Lieutenant Jehu Hay.

For decades after the siege the only written account came from a diary written by Robert Navarre, a prominent Frenchman. In 1860 a document known as *Diary of the Siege of Detroit*, written by an Englishman, but unsigned, appeared in print. The diary refers repeatedly to Hay's participation in British encounters with the surrounding Indians. By decoding portions of the diary and comparing it with letters, historians identified the anonymous writer as Lieutenant Hay.[10] Why he chose not to acknowledge authorship is unknown. It may have been safer not to take credit for the account of a controversial encounter.

Hay served heroically in the battles, as the British held off Pontiac's forces. Reinforcements arrived some months after the siege began and rescued the fort.[11] Ironically, Hay later built a close working relationship with Indian tribes of the Ohio valley as part of waging war against the Americans.

A year after the siege Jehu put down roots in Detroit and married Marie Julie Reaume, 16. On May 8, 1869, Marie Julie gave birth to John Hay, the second son. Church records are incomplete regarding the Hay family, and no record of the marriage exists.

Hay's involvement with the Reaumes might also explain a major influence on Hay's career. Members of the Reaume family were on intimate terms with Indian tribes. Charles Reaume, an elder brother of Marie Julie, spent 50 years as an interpreter in the British Indian Department. Jean Baptiste, another brother, engaged in Indian trade.[12] Whether this made an impression on Jehu or not, in May, 1765, he applied for an appointment as Commissioner of Indian Trade at Detroit, and got the job a year later. In this position Hay developed a close relationship with Governor Hamilton, and became involved in activities with Indian tribes that would mark him for life.

In the years leading to the American Revolution, Hamilton managed the Detroit outpost with relatively few British soldiers. He augmented these forces with friendly Indian tribes that he encouraged to assault American settlers. Jehu's job included distributing gifts as payment to the Indians. Hamilton became the most hated Englishman in the eyes of frontier Americans, with Jehu not far behind. But Hay also had enemies in the British officer ranks among those who differed with the policy of encouraging Indian atrocities. Having performed duties as commissioner of trade with Indians to suit Governor Hamilton, Jehu became deputy superintendent of the Indian Department, retaining the rank of major in the militia.

After capitulation to George Rogers Clark at Vincennes in 1778, Hay and Hamilton were imprisoned in Virginia until 1781. The two departed for England after being traded for prisoners held by the British. During this period Hamilton wrote of his experiences in captivity and referred to Jehu's lengthy absence from Detroit: "Major Hay has been absent from a numerous family three years and half, I should be utterly undeserving . . . did I not pass over in silence his meritorious services and suffering, during so long so painfull, and so ignominious a captivity."[13] Jehu's son John, then twelve years old, had not seen his father since age nine.

Neither Hamilton nor Hay retired from public life. Technically speaking, Hamilton retained the title and responsibilities as lieutenant governor of Detroit but he showed no interest in returning. In part out of sympathy for the depredations he suffered in captivity, Hamilton received appointment as lieutenant governor of Canada. That left open the position at Detroit. In consideration, too, for Hay's service to England, he was named lieutenant governor of Detroit on April 23, 1782.[14]

After the appointment Jehu still could not get home to see his wife and family. He arrived at Quebec in June to find an uproar. In Hay's absence other officers had taken over military and administrative duties in Detroit. Colonel Arent Schuyler de Peyster, the military commandant, claimed Jehu was subordinate to him in military rank and refused to remain in the military position if Hay became the civil government leader. He wrote his commanding general that he "did not wish to have anything to do with Mr. Hay."[15]

While officials tried to find a suitable assignment for DePeyster, Hay languished at Canadian military posts until November. DePeyster was reassigned to Niagara, and Jehu got permission to proceed to Detroit. He started home but became ill and returned to Montreal until spring of 1784. Hay finally reached Detroit in July, more than two years after his appointment.[16]

Hay's lingering illness together with difficulties in assuming the position made him irritable and unpleasant in dealings with associates and superiors. In letters to Hamilton and friendly associates, Hay complained continuously about restrictions on his authority, and referred to himself as nothing more than a "cypher." Hay said he detected an "air of distrust and want of Confidence" in his situation and in dealings with officials. His correspondence described how the lowliest officer had more control of troops than did the governor.[17] On August 2, 1785, after a brief illness, Jehu Hay died about age 47. His widow was 37, the oldest child nearly 18. John Hay was 16.

The death of his father had serious impact on young John Hay. Not only had John just begun to re-establish a relationship with his often-absent father, but negative attitudes toward Jehu and the family among soldiers and citizens in Detroit left a pall. These sad circumstances may have convinced John to stay away from Detroit. At a minimum, John needed to find work so as not to be a burden on his mother. He now had to find his own way, hoping that the father's life experiences, good and bad, had provided useful lessons.

Details of John Hay's life until 1793 when he arrived in Cahokia are incomplete. He apparently attended college in Canada, where he received an education in the classics. With encouragement of his family, and as a result of schooling, Hay became fluent in Latin, French and English. Later he learned Spanish.[18]

From age 14, which predates his father's death by two years, John Hay worked at a commercial house in Montreal, the center of Canadian and British fur trade. At the merchants' desk he kept books for a firm owned by Scottish traders. While in Montreal he became familiar with Scotsman Isaac Todd and partners, who managed one of the largest and most prosperous trading houses in Montreal with major activities in the central regions of Canada. Hay's first contact with Andrew Todd, nephew of Isaac Todd occurred during that time.

A desk job with a trading firm for someone as young as Hay made him impatient for adventure and excitement away from the office. He wanted to join others who made overland and water voyages for trade with Indians. John got his chance when his mentors agreed to finance an excursion to south central Canada known as the Red River/Assiniboine river country. Today the Red River cuts the boundary between Minnesota and North Dakota, and flows northward into Lake Winnipeg in the Canadian province of Manitoba. The Assiniboine, draining an area in southwest Manitoba, flows into the Red River at the city of Winnipeg.

Trade in that part of North America, then controlled by England-based Hudson's Bay Company, and Montreal interests, consisted mostly of delivering goods and gifts to Indians, and returning with furs for the European markets. Indian tribes in the northern plains had years of trade experience with each other before Europeans arrived. Cautious fur traders supplemented existing tribal trade routes, rather than try to replace them.

Reaching Red River country and the northern tribes from Montreal took months of difficult overland travel, much of it by canoe, through barren and remote territory fraught with danger of attack by unfriendly Indians. It is doubtful that young Hay made the risky trip by himself but there is no record of how many accompanied him. John Reynolds said the Montreal employers equipped him with items to be sold to Indians, such as blankets, flints, powder, bullets, knives and paints.[19] A round trip probably took Hay the better part of two years.

While Hay worked trade routes for Montreal interests, the British undertook a large-scale push to extend the fur trade business west of present-day Michigan and Wisconsin. The French had faded from the trade picture by the late 1780s and the Spanish did not have resources to mount trade efforts in Upper Louisiana and Missouri River country. Consequently, the opportunistic English figuratively galloped into the vacuum. Montreal trading companies formed a confederation called the North West Company, and joined the Hudson's Bay Company in competition for the lucrative fur trade. These competing companies had their eyes on the Red River country and the Pacific coast beyond.[20]

British controlled the upper Mississippi River and central Canada trade because they were smart and aggressive and did not fear the Spanish. The lure of a treasure in furs inspired traders to win the favor of Indians by offering superior goods, and England and Europe provided the world's largest market. However, on the horizon loomed a final agreement ending the war between the United States and England. As a result America would receive lands in the Upper Mississippi region—now Michigan, Wisconsin and Minnesota—and the Missouri River would be open to increased competitive trade. The British wanted a secure foothold in lands west of the Mississippi before a final peace treaty with the United States.[21]

These events are significant to the story of Lewis and Clark. Indian tribes and the British and Canadians lived and hunted near the Missouri River as it winds through central and western North Dakota—the eventual route of the Corps of Discovery. Tribes in the vicinity included the Mandans that lived at the "big bend" in the Missouri River. Lewis and Clark needed information about the hostility or friendliness of Indians. This made Hay's experience near the Red River essential to the captains' preparation, in combination with documents of recent explorers of the Missouri. He knew the tribes, how to trade with them, and the circumstances under which they would remain friendly.

Sometime during John Hay's work in the fur trade he joined the North West Company as an employee, renewing contact with Montreal colleague Andrew Todd. The enterprising Scot had eyes for the Cahokia trade and activities along the middle and lower Mississippi River. He faced a major roadblock, however, because Spain controlled the Mississippi trade route and barred the English and Americans from participating.[22] Grabbing a piece of that action required creativity and eventually included John Hay.

The importance of Hay's work with Todd is clear. Accompanied by Todd, Hay, in his early 20s, went from the loneliness and isolation of trading for others in the wilderness, to a partnership located in one of the trade centers on the Mississippi. We don't know what Todd saw in Hay. He may have been looking for a young and energetic man willing to take on risk. Or it may have been the depth of Hay's experience. In spite of Hay's youth he had worked in the trade business for more than 10 years. The partnership allowed time for Todd to cut the deals, and his young partner to care for the details.

Hay needed a change. According to John Reynolds, "Mr. Hay did not make a fortune on his outfit; but he saw the world, even if it were in the north-west. In that region, he formed an acquaintance with a Mr. Todd, a merchant of considerable celebrity ship. They determined to establish their main store in Cahokia and send out in boats, or otherwise, goods into the Indian country."[23] Hay headed for Cahokia sometime in 1793, anticipating partnership in a firm named Hay and Todd. He started for Illinois country with one Indian companion. From the Red River, they entered St. Peter's River (Minnesota River) and descended to the Mississippi. They stopped at Prairie du Chien where Hay left his companion and went on to Cahokia alone.[24]

Now a businessman in Cahokia, Hay recorded at least one more journey to the Red River wilderness. At the beginning of his partnership with Todd in 1794, Hay and a party made a fur trade journey deep into the Red River region to trade with Indians. He kept a journal that began June 27 and ended October 28.[25] It gives distances traveled, descriptions of the landscape and a sense of the arduous journey required to reach the Indian fur trade. Voyageurs often rowed in a canoe from dawn to dark, and made countless portages where streams were not navigable. When out of the canoe the voyageurs carried packs of goods weighing at least 90 pounds and often three times as much.

The party left Fort Mackinac where Todd had headquarters, headed north to Sault Ste. Marie and turned west along the southern shore of Lake Superior. Hay and companions followed the lake across the upper peninsula of Michigan, to the north shore of Wisconsin and finished the lake trek near the location of Duluth, Minnesota. At that point Hay and travelers began a difficult journey west to the Red River.[26] They saw no other human beings, although they traveled through hostile Sioux Indian territory.

Hay's party headed due west from Lake Superior across hilly and rocky terrain and reached Big Sandy Lake, a 50-mile trip that took almost three weeks. Sandy Lake later became an important location in the fur trade of the Northwest.

Near the lake they picked up the Mississippi River, not far below its beginnings in northern Minnesota, and followed it south to near present-day Brainerd, Minnesota, at the confluence with the Crow Wing River. They turned westward again along the Crow Wing to the Leaf River. Hay followed the river to Leaf Lake and then to Otter Tail Lake a few miles east of today's Fergus Falls, Minnesota. The party continued west on Otter Tail River and joined the Red River below the current location of Fargo, North Dakota. It required three more weeks of travel to winter camp in southwest Manitoba along the Souris River.[27]

The Souris flows into the Assiniboine River in southwest Manitoba Province in a thickly wooded area where bears and other wildlife proliferated. Hay also recalled seeing vacant North West Company forts and Hudson's Bay facilities on the main rivers. He estimated winter camp on the Souris about 400 miles from the Red River. This would put the camp in Montana or extreme southeastern Saskatchewan Province. The trade routes with Indians on the Souris included the Mandans, who provided corn and other grains for the northern tribes, in return for buffalo meat, robes and clothing.

While Hay headed to Souris River country, Todd had adventures of his own in attempting to trade along the Mississippi River. An unfortunate encounter on the Mississippi demonstrated to Todd the necessity of working out a trade arrangement with the Spanish. At the confluence of the Des Moines River with the Mississippi, Spanish authorities seized a load of Todd's goods headed from Mackinac to New Orleans. Todd protested to the Spanish through British officials in Canada, but Baron de Carondelet, then governor of Upper Louisiana, ignored the concerns.[28] He observed that the British had engaged in illegal trade on the Mississippi for some time, and Todd simply got caught.

The Spanish embargo threatened Todd's business expansion ideas, and drove him to consider a legal way to trade on the river. This brought him in contact with the leading traders of Spanish territory: the Chouteau brothers, Charles Gratiot, and Jacques Clamorgan. The Chouteau brothers and Gratiot are familiar to this story. Background on Jacques Clamorgan is necessary to complete the picture of alliances that opened the Missouri River to organized exploration before Lewis and Clark, and added to John Hay's further education.

Clamorgan is remembered as endowed with a creative imagination, the gift of gab and a driving ambition to develop western trade routes. He speculated and operated—often deviously—throughout the Mississippi Valley during the 1780s and 1790s. His biographer, Abraham Nasatir, described Clamorgan, " . . . as a slave dealer, fur trader, merchant, financier, land speculator."[29] At the time of Hay and Todd, Clamorgan operated as a Spanish subject in Upper Louisiana. He had grand dreams of capturing the Mississippi, Santa Fe and Missouri fur trade, and he wanted more than anything to be accepted on business and social grounds among the wealthy of St. Louis. The Chouteaus and Gratiot found Clamorgan too coarse for their circles.[30]

Todd's appearance on the scene with financial resources helped all parties achieve their goals. Todd needed Clamorgan to bring the Spanish to the table and grant him rights to trade on the rivers. The Chouteaus and Gratiot could not resist being part of ventures that opened the Missouri River, and they wanted the benefit of Todd's connections to the Canadian trade. Finally, the Spanish saw Todd as someone who might help them push the British out of the Upper Mississippi and Upper Missouri regions.

In 1794 Clamorgan persuaded the Spanish to give Todd exclusive trade rights on the Mississippi. To move matters along, Todd agreed to become a Spanish subject. Spain granted Todd a trade monopoly on the Mississippi and Missouri, with Clamorgan as a partner.[31] Todd, who had the confidence of the Chouteaus from earlier business encounters, brought the St. Louis traders and Clamorgan together.

These alliances led immediately to plans for a Missouri River exploration in the mid-1790s. Through an organization called the "Company of Explorers of the Upper Missouri"—known generally as the Missouri Company—operated by Clamorgan, the group put Todd's money to work.[32] The company first backed explorer Jean Baptiste Truteau on the Missouri in 1795, but he failed to get much beyond Nebraska country. A second exploration failed to eclipse Truteau.[33]

The Missouri Company then financed an ambitious effort by explorers James Mackay and John Thomas Evans that pushed to the Mandan villages in 1796. Although each of these efforts failed to fulfill the objective of reaching the Pacific, they provided valuable information that eventually reached Lewis and Clark.

The Spanish granted Todd exclusive commerce with the Indian nations to the north of the Ohio and on the Missouri on June

11, 1796. As part of the understanding, Spain paid for a portion of Todd's cargo that had been seized three years earlier. Five months later Todd went to New Orleans to arrange for shipment of furs to Europe, and to see about matters involving his office. He planned a return to the Illinois country soon thereafter. The great promise of Missouri and Mississippi river trade was about to land in the laps of Hay and Todd.

Todd arrived in New Orleans during a yellow fever epidemic. Fifteen days later he was stricken, and five days after that he died.[34] His death sent shock waves through the intricate network of companies and agreements he had with Hay, Clamorgan, the Spanish, and fur traders in St. Louis and New Orleans. People familiar with the arrangements predicted the financial collapse of virtually everything, resulting from the inability of Clamorgan to pay off loans to Todd's estate. Isaac Todd, executor of his nephew's estate and heir, placed John Hay in charge of cleaning up Todd's affairs in the Illinois country.

Hay stepped into a mess. Every Todd creditor clamored for money from the estate, and the estate sought the payoff of loans Todd had extended. Events pushed Clamorgan to the edge of bankruptcy, but miraculously he avoided total failure. At one point in 1798, Clamorgan accused Hay of fleeing St. Louis to avoid paying a debt.[35] Nothing came of the accusation, but it illustrates the confusion and emotion surrounding Todd's death.

Hay's career as a merchant and trader ended with his partner's death. Instead of moving on to a similar opportunity along the Mississippi Valley, which he easily could have done, Hay decided to remain in the Illinois country. He never entered private business on a large scale again.

Tragedy always seemed just around the corner for Hay. In the midst of Todd's deal making and Hay's return from the north country, his mother Marie Julie Reaume Hay died in Detroit in 1795.[36] There is nothing to indicate John returned in time to participate in ceremonies. She was buried "beneath the second pew" of Ste. Anne's Church in Detroit, adjoining her husband Jehu.

A major change in governance of the Illinois country occurred in 1795 which, along with the death of Andrew Todd a year later, had a profound impact on John Hay. Beginning in 1790 the Northwest territorial governor, Arthur St. Clair, tried to find an efficient system for governing settlements along the Mississippi River. The governor first placed Illinois in a county he immodestly named St. Clair, that covered most of Northwest Territory. Concentration of administrative responsibility in Kaskaskia presented huge problems, and angered people in Cahokia. That experiment failed, and in 1795 Governor St. Clair split off Randolph County to the south. He chose Kaskaskia as the capital of Randolph County, and Cahokia as the capital of St. Clair.

With the changes came the challenge of establishing a governance system, including courts and administration. This required the services of people who could make judgments and decisions in an environment where government was unfamiliar and unfriendly for many. In St. Clair County that responsibility fell largely to William St. Clair, a cousin of Governor St. Clair and a son of the Earl of Roslin in England.

William St. Clair came to Cahokia from Detroit in 1790, having refused to serve in the British militia and recruit Indians to fight against people in the Illinois country.[37] Governor St. Clair appointed his cousin to high judicial positions soon after the declaration of St. Clair County. William served as chief clerk of the common pleas, with jurisdiction over civil law, and as recorder of deeds.

When Arthur St. Clair created Randolph and St. Clair counties in 1795, he appointed William chief judge of the common pleas, and judge of probate. Hay and William St. Clair developed a working relationship and friendship, hastened by the death of Todd. Hay understudied William St. Clair in the administrative positions, putting to use skills he had acquired in Montreal and working with Todd.

While his work status remained in flux, Hay married Marguerite Pouport, a French Creole from Cahokia in 1797.[38] During a life together of more than four decades they reared a large family, several members of which had distinguished public careers in Belleville and St. Clair County. One daughter married into the Chouteau family in St. Louis. Son John became St. Clair County prosecuting attorney, a major in the Union army during the Civil War, congressman, and mayor of Belleville.

As so often happened in Hay's life, dramatic events brought him to another turning point on the road to his encounter with Lewis and Clark. William St. Clair died early in 1797. Hay was one of the subscribing witnesses to St. Clair's will, and executor.[39] Soon after William's death Governor St. Clair elevated Hay to several important positions, including clerk of the court of common pleas, clerk of orphans' court, clerk of the court of quarter sessions with responsibilities for criminal law, recorder of deeds and treasurer of St. Clair County.[40] Although positions and titles changed over the years, Hay held important county and regional government positions until his death in 1843.

Over those years of service to local government, Hay earned the affectionate title of "generalissimo of the pen."[41] The name reflected respect for his ability to write wills and contracts, and assist merchants with their records. His liberal education, extraordinary for someone of that time, gave him a command of English to go along with the French he learned from his mother. The combination launched Hay on a career that put him in touch with the highest-ranking officials, politicians and average citizens in the territory.

Hay's new jobs plunged him into the thick of territorial politics as the nineteenth century began. In 1800 Congress established Indiana Territory, which included what would later become the state of Illinois. In 1801 William Henry Harrison took over as governor. Once again, Hay became the beneficiary of change and its handmaiden, opportunity. Harrison and Hay became acquainted early in the governor's tenure. From his administrative position, Hay kept Harrison informed of issues and personalities in the Illinois country. Harrison quickly recognized the importance of having Hay on his team, and Hay understood the reality of who appointed him to leadership positions.

The relationship between Harrison and Hay took shape between 1801 and 1805. As the region struggled with whether to legalize slavery and how to meet the demand for more self-government, Harrison became the center of controversy. Hay remained loyal to Harrison although friends and associates in Illinois divided into opposing camps over the governor's actions. Not until 1805, when Illinois sentiment began to turn sharply against Harrison, did Hay take issue with the governor on any major issue.[42] At the time Lewis and Clark arrived, Hay and the governor held each other in highest regard. Harrison also had the respect of the two captains.

The governor demonstrated his confidence in Hay on two occasions in 1804. The first concerned the transfer ceremony in St. Louis for the Louisiana Purchase. While wholly symbolic because the official ceremony had occurred in New Orleans three months earlier, the event had great emotional importance to the French in St. Louis and the region. Although the Spanish had controlled French territory, technically it still belonged to the French. The ceremony acknowledged both the French and Spanish claims and took two days to accomplish. Dignitaries from far and wide attended the event.

Unable to be on hand for the ceremony, Harrison asked Hay to represent St. Clair County as an official delegate.[43] Hay stood with the elite of the Illinois country and St. Louis, the Chouteaus and Gratiot, Lewis and Clark, and many others. As witness to the historic events in St. Louis, Hay could only have thought back to his roots as an English subject, his father's record as a warrior against the American rebels and experiences with imprisonment in Virginia, and his own passage to governmental leadership in Cahokia.

Once the transfer occurred, Captain Stoddard, who Lewis and Clark first met at Kaskaskia, remained on temporary duty as military and civil commander of Upper Louisiana until August, when the full administrative takeover occurred. On that occasion Harrison made an official trip to Illinois. His entourage traveled overland from Vincennes to Cahokia, where Harrison met Hay and other local officials. Harrison asked Hay to accompany him to St. Louis and assume an official role in helping with the administrative transfer of Louisiana to the U.S. The Cahokian joined Harrison's group and worked with people in St. Louis.[44]

Harrison continued to show respect for Hay when, a year later, he appointed him to a term on the territorial council, the legislative body similar to a senate. That step forward on the governing scale brought Hay to the forefront of politics in Illinois country, a role he may not have relished.

Hay served one three-year term on the council, and Harrison re-appointed him for a second in 1808. During those years the battles with Harrison over the governor's opposition to the creation of Illinois Territory damaged relationships throughout the region. There is nothing to indicate a breach between Harrison and Hay before 1808 when Hay resigned from the council. He stepped down just as the territorial legislature reached the brink of a showdown with Harrison over separation from Indiana Territory. By then many Illinois country officials who had remained loyal to Harrison changed course and supported establishment of Illinois Territory.[45]

Hay continued performing in many important roles as Illinois headed toward statehood in the years after 1809, and the establishment of Illinois Territory. His appointment in 1814 as one of a handful of people chosen to select a site for the new county seat of Belleville should not have surprised anyone. He already had earned a reputation as one of St. Clair County's first citizens. Hay is credited with naming the community. "Let's name it what we want it to be, 'beautiful city,' and for memory's sake, let's put it in French— Belle Ville," he is quoted as saying.[46]

He became Belleville's second permanent inhabitant when county government moved to that location. Hay held numerous appointive positions throughout his long career in St. Clair County's public life, many at the same time. He often said he needed to fill as many jobs as possible to earn a decent living and provide for his large family. Apparently he juggled those positions effectively because whenever a term expired, Hay's employers always reappointed him.

Hay's wife died in 1842, in Belleville, and he died a year later. The local newspaper said in its obituary of Hay:

> Few men were so well known and so much respected. The whole country mourns the departure of a public spirited citizen and warm-hearted, kind and benevolent man. As a magistrate, he was distinguished by unwavering partiality, by love of justice, and the most scrupulous . . . discharge of his duties, and an efficient and laborious attention to the business of his offices . . . We believe all who knew him loved him, and that he had not a personal enemy on earth.[47]

Writing less than 10 years after Hay's death, Reynolds said of his longtime friend: "Mr. Hay was never idle or indolent, but worked while life lasted. He was not wealthy, but he enjoyed a good degree of happiness in his quiet home with his wife. He raised a large and respectable family, and died as he had lived, beloved and respected by all who knew him."[48]

Because of Hay's long life, many of his greatest accomplishments occurred after meeting Lewis and Clark. That makes his accomplishments by 1803 even more impressive. He had gone further in public life than most others at the tender age of 34. He survived pitfalls that would have destroyed people of weaker convictions and less self-confidence. Noteworthy as his accomplishments were in Cahokia, Belleville and St. Clair County, the memory of Hay lives through mentions of contributions to the Corps of Discovery in Lewis's letters and Clark's field notes, and in the discoveries of historians.

While much of the activity among Hay, Lewis and Clark is recorded, one meeting in particular is not part of the chronicles. It may have been one of the most important for Hay and the captains, although we have to imagine what it was like. This was the first meeting of William Clark and John Hay in the Illinois country—whether it occurred on Clark's visit in 1797 or when the Corps arrived in 1803. In retrospect, it carried the weight of high drama, given what occurred twenty or more years before in Vincennes at the surrender of Hamilton and Jehu Hay to George Rogers Clark.

Surely Hay knew the story of his father's surrender to George Rogers Clark, and the ignominy of imprisonment in Virginia. When he first heard the story in Detroit from Jehu's lips, John must have recognized the hatred his father felt for Americans, and especially for George Rogers Clark. There were many opportunities for William Clark to hear first hand from his older brother about the British soldiers captured at Fort Sackville, including Jehu Hay. The fact remained that John Hay and Lewis and Clark might never have met as they did if General Clark had not succeeded.

William Clark and John Hay got past these family conflicts because it was not in the nature of either man to be spiteful. Neither lived on the reputation of his relative. Historians have suggested that conflict on the frontier, even to the point of open warfare, was such a part of life that hard feelings rarely were carried from one generation to the next.[49] That will have to stand as explanations for their behavior.

With the exception of the Corps of Discovery members, no one seemed more engaged in work of the expedition than Hay. Lewis called on Hay when he needed an interpreter on many visits to St. Louis. Hay provided accommodations for Lewis when the captain spent days and weeks away from the encampment. Hay shared specific information from his own experiences on the Red River and in Souris River country. He translated journals and interpreted maps of those who had gone up the Missouri River before Lewis and Clark. He invited the captains to engagements in St. Louis, where they had the ear of the community's political and social elite. This was John Hay's supreme moment, bringing all those years in Canada and on frontiers to bear for Lewis and Clark.

11.

On to Camp Dubois

Beginning in May, 1804, Lewis and Clark spent most of the following two years and four months—except for a portion of the return trip from the Pacific—in the company of each other. Historians attribute success of the expedition to how well the captains worked together during those months. The full story is, it appears they worked well together even when separated because each knew his role in the mission, and accepted full responsibility.

Lewis's departure from Clark and the party on December 3 at Kaskaskia started a period of nearly five and a half months when they spent much of the time in separate locations. In discussions coming down the Ohio River, and while fighting their way up river against the current of the Mississippi, Lewis and Clark must have agreed on their duties for winter camp. As it turned out, Lewis worked the crowd in St. Louis, Cahokia and environs, and Clark kept the Wood River camp operating for the Corps of Discovery from December 1803, to May 1804.

In many respects the truly hard work of preparing for the expedition began when the captains parted company at Kaskaskia. Surviving records, including the notes of Clark and correspondence by Lewis, leave little doubt that they needed every hour of the time to complete their work before starting the journey on May 14. Lewis and Clark's years on the frontier prepared them well for the tasks ahead, but neither of them had worked against a dead-line for such an ambitious project.

With Lewis in St. Louis, Clark and a group now numbering in the 20s stopped overnight near the present city of East St. Louis on December 10. The following night, concluding their last full day on the Mississippi before arriving at winter camp, they stopped on an island thought to be Cabaret Island or Wood Island, oppo-site the location today of Granite City.

Jarrot probably gave them directions to his land along the Wood River, or drew a map to indicate where he owned land adja-cent to the small river that flowed into the Mississippi from the Illinois country. Clark, the boats, and men arrived at the location seventeen and a half river miles above Cahokia Landing during a storm about 2 p.m. on December 12. Clark wrote this descrip-tion:

> Nearly opposite the Missouries I came to in the mouth of a little River called Wood River, about 2 oClock and imediately after I had landed the N W wind which had been blowing all day increased to a Storm which was accompanied by Hail & Snow, & the wind Continued to blow from the Same point with violence. Not soon after I had landed two Canoos of Potowautomi Indians Came upon the other Side and landed formed their Camp and three of them in a Small Canoo Came across when the waves was so high & wind blowing with violence that I expected their Canoo would Certounly fill with water or turn over, but to my astonish-ment found on their landing that they were all Drunk and their Canoo had not received any water. The hunders which I had sent out to examine the Countrey in Deferent derections, returned with Turkeys & opossums and informed me the Countrey was butifull and had great appearance of Gaim.[1]

For a century and a half from the time of their encampment in 1803 until 1953, the world knew little about activities at Camp Dubois. The only sources were correspondence of the captains with Jefferson, and scattered reports such as those about the St. Louis ceremony for transfer of Louisiana territory to the United States. There were no newspapers in the Illinois country at that time.

Fortunately for the record, Clark wrote informal accounts, known as field notes, during the months of winter camp starting December 13. Their discovery in 1953 is explained in publications edited and written by historians Ernest Staples Osgood and Paul Russell Cutright.[2] Yale University Press published Osgood's editing of Clark's notes in 1962. They were casual notes, written on scratch paper, which became separated from the journals.

Unlike the official journals, Clark wrote the field notes on 12 loose sheets of different sized paper. In editing, Osgood found the order difficult to follow as the captain also used the same sheets for miscellaneous notes.[3] Clark made frequent entries while at Camp Dubois, but he made no entries while in St. Louis or other locations. Some of his scribblings never have been explained. Imperfect, sketchy and disorganized as the account is, it provides the only detail of nearly five months in winter camp while the party prepared for the journey.

Shortly after leaving the campsite near East St. Louis on December 10, Clark and party had passed into what is now Madison County, Illinois. Official declaration of that county did not occur until 1812. Compared to settlement of the American Bottom from Kaskaskia to Cahokia, the area north of the settlements was sparsely settled. Scattered individual farms existed, but no clusters of settlements. The earliest immigrants to the region arrived in the 1790s and by 1800 a few people had moved to an area called Goshen, which is near the location of Collinsville, well west of the Mississippi River.[4]

Among the first arrivals in Goshen were children and relatives of the Whiteside family who settled originally between Cahokia and Kaskaskia.[5] Whitesides, probably some from Goshen and others from Whiteside Station, showed up periodically at winter camp, although it is not easy to determine which members of the family visited. We can only guess that William Whiteside, the Indian fighter, made the journey on several occasions. There were so many Whitesides in the vicinity of Camp Dubois that it is also likely that his son, William B. Whiteside, stopped with his father and may have visited on his own.

Whitesides visited the camp on January 2, January 4 and January 31, according to Clark's notes. On January 2, Clark wrote "Cap Whitesides Came to See me & his Son, and some countrey people . . . Mr. Whitesides says a no. of young men in his Neghborhood wishes to accompany Capt Lewis & myself on the Expdts. . . ."[6] Recalling that Clark had met the Whitesides either on his 1797 journey to Illinois country or when he and the party passed along the Mississippi not far from Whiteside Station, the reference is most likely to the family leader William who came from Virginia. The mention of a son could mean any one of four belonging to William Whiteside. The eldest, William B. Whiteside, made his home in Goshen, as did younger brother Uel. The other visitors with Whiteside may have been the family of James Gillham, a nearby farmer.[7]

The January 4 entry referred to "Whitesides" selling beef to the commissary. This may have been William, William B. or Uel, the second oldest son who moved close to present Collinsville. On January 31 Clark stated, " . . . Mr. Whitesides & Chittele crossed from the opposit Side of the Mississippi. . . ." Again, the mentioned Whiteside could have been any of the three older men, and either Seth or Richard Chitwood, brothers of Isabella Elizabeth Whiteside, a sister-in-law of William.

As Clark moved northward on the Mississippi from East St. Louis the river paralleled an extension of the American Bottom. About six miles north of St. Louis and just a few miles south of winter camp was Six-Mile Prairie, one of the earliest gatherings of settlers in Madison County. In 1803 a few people farmed there.[8] Land speculators had begun carving up choice locations in that

part of St. Clair County. Those most active in accumulating land
are familiar to our story for the huge number of acres they acquired in the 1790s and early 1800s. John Edgar and William
Morrison expanded their land holdings northward, but Nicholas
Jarrot had a big jump on them, particularly in what is now the
southern portion of Madison County. On Six-Mile Prairie,
Morrison land was farmed by an employee of Bryan and Morrison,
the trading firm, which had stores in Kaskaskia and Cahokia.

Patrick Heneberry—the last name is spelled various ways by
the captains and early historians—farmed the Morrison site. According to account books at the Cahokia store of Bryan and
Morrison, Heneberry performed a number of activities for the firm.
He made early contact with the party and provided food and tools
from Morrison's farm.

Lewis wrote in a letter to Clark on December 17, "Hennebury
informed me that he would be at Morrison's farm today or Tomor-
row, and that he knew a person in the neighborhood who had a
whip-saw, and that he would go with any person you might send
to this gentleman, and prevail on him to let us have the uce of the
saw. You can obtain corn for the horses by application to
Hennebury or any person who has the care of Morrison's farm."[9]
Six days later Clark wrote, "I Send to Mr Morrisons farm for a
Teem&Corn, which arivd about 3 oClock. . . ."[10] Corn was a major crop along the American Bottom.

Heneberry also may have had information of value to Clark. In
notes of January 1, Clark said he talked with Heneberry, also a
blacksmith, who had traveled "far to the North, & Visited the
Man'd on Missouris. . . ."[11] The captains sought information about
the Mandan Indians and the Red River area of North Dakota. It is
doubtful if Heneberry had as much credibility as other sources,
which would explain why he is not mentioned again in that context. Heneberry disappeared from the area between 1805 and 1809
with an amount due to Bryan and Morrison of $158.85.[12]

The Gillham family had an early 1800s stake in the Six-Mile
vicinity and could have provided goods to soldiers from Camp

Dubois. Of the many accounts of early arrivals, the Gillham story ranks among the most dramatic.[13] The first Gillham to settle in Madison County was James, who came to the Illinois country from Kentucky in 1794 in search of his wife and children who were captives of Kickapoo Indians. Two French guides and interpreters took Gillham to visit the Kickapoo settlement and found his wife and children alive and well. Gillham paid a ransom through a Cahokia trader and all returned to the home in Kentucky. Gillham liked Illinois country so much the family returned three years later to settle on Six-Mile Prairie.

In the early 1800s Gillham farmed on the prairie and operated a ferry on the Mississippi River opposite the mouth of the Missouri, apparently after the expedition left winter quarters. A local historian says Gillham bought the ferry site from Jacob Whiteside, a nephew of William Whiteside, three weeks before Clark and the crew arrived. The location became known later as "Gillham's Landing."[14]

Scholars, curiosity seekers, and local historians have swarmed over Madison County in recent years attempting to locate the exact site of winter camp, and determine approximately where the site would be today. With a few exceptions, almost every sleuth agrees that the campsite was on the south side of the Wood River when the party arrived, although Clark did not say specifically in his notes. Local historian Everett L. Sparks wrote the following upon his investigation:

> I found where, on December 15, 1803, Clark clearly identified the location of Wood River Camp: "I cut a road to the prairey 2490 yards east." He did not say 2,500 yards, so I assume he measured the distance. The edge of the prairie is shown on the 1808 Survey of Wood River Township, and 2,490 yards west of the prairie would place the campsite today [1988] on the Missouri state side of the Mississippi River roughly two miles up the Mississippi from the present

mouth of the Missouri. Today most people agree with this location."[15]

Sparks added, "As one stands today at the Lewis and Clark Memorial on the Illinois side of the Mississippi River, and looks across the Mississippi to the Missouri side, the land he sees was, in 1804, Illinois soil."

Roy E. Appleman, of the National Park Service, wrote about the site, "During some 170 years of changing river channels in the vicinity, the site of Camp Wood has shifted from the south bank of the Wood River at its junction with the Mississippi River . . . to the opposite bank of the Mississippi. The Missouri at its mouth has pushed southward; the Mississippi has moved eastward; and a new channel has been dredged for the Wood River."[16]

An article by Illinois writer Robert D. Fietsam, Jr., published in 1996, reached a similar conclusion to that of Sparks. He said because of changes in the rivers, the original campsite is about "three miles north of the present-day Wood River Historical Marker site."[17]

The impact of erosion from flooding of the Missouri and Mississippi rivers over the decades is hard to imagine today. Sparks wrote, "At the confluence, the Missouri clobbers the Mississippi. The Missouri comes in at a normal seven miles per hour while the maximum velocity of the Mississippi during the 1973 flood was only four mph [miles per hour]; normally it flows at less than two mph. At flood time the Missouri takes over the full width of the riverbed and even more at the present Lewis and Clark Memorial."[18]

Early in the nineteenth century rivers, without levees, found their own channels and had room to spread, causing significant changes in river courses. The greatest damage to riverbanks on the Mississippi occurred during the "great floods" in 1826 and 1844. Either of these floods could have wiped out everything around the mouth of the Wood River. Sparks wrote that the mouth of the Missouri River remained in approximately the same location from 1804 until about 1865, then began movement downstream to its present location, about six miles south.[19]

The Corps' campsite afforded Clark an ideal vantage point for studying moods of the rivers and human traffic. Mississippi Valley scholar John Francis McDermott studied a sketch made by Clark, which shows the campsite on the south bank of the Wood River and termed it a perfect location for observing changes in the Missouri River.[20] For example, on January 3, Clark wrote that it was "a Verry Cold blustering day . . . the View up the Missourie appeared Dredfull, as the wind blew off the Sand with fury as to Almost darken that part of the atmespear . . . I am told that an old french fort was once built on the opsd side of the river from me, and that Some remains of the clearing is yet to be seen. . . ."[21]

Further evidence of the location comes from Clark's description of the camp location from a letter written January 15, to his brother-in-law Major William C. Croghan, who lived in Kentucky. Not known for his eloquence or flowery prose, Clark did himself proud on this occasion:

> My situation is as comfortable as could be expected in the woods, & on the frontiers; the Country back of me is butifull beyond discription; a rich bottom well timbered, from one to three mile wide, from the river to a Prarie; which runs nearly parrilal to the river from about three miles above me, to Kaskaskia and is from three to 7 miles wide, with gradual rises and several streams of runing water, and good Mill seats; This Prarie has settlements on its edges from Kahoka within three miles of this place. The Missouri which mouths imedeately opposet me is the river we intend assending as soon as the weather will permit. This Great river which seems to dispute the preeminence with the Mississippi, coms in at right angles from the West, and forces its great sheets of muddy Ice (which is now running) against the Eastern bank. . . .[22]

The disagreement regarding the location to which the campsite shifted over the decades is primarily between interests in Mis-

souri and Illinois. Illinois officials and residents firmly believe the
site now is near Hartford and that is where a state historic site has
been established. National Lewis and Clark organization officials
have designated the Illinois site as the point from which the expedition began.

A few settlers near the campsite have been identified, although
Clark's notes are imprecise. Two vague references, one in Clark's
notes of January 6, and one from Sergeant John Ordway's journal
of September 23, 1806, the day the journey ended, hint of a neigh-
bor closer to the campsite than any others.

Clark wrote, "I order in those men who had fought got Drunk
& neglected Duty to go and build a hut for a Wo[man] who prom-
ises to wash &Sow &c."[23] Then Ordway wrote in his journal two
and a half years later, " . . . here [the campsite] we found a widdow
woman who we left here & has a plantation under tollarable good
way Since we have been on the Expedition."[24]

Further clues as to the location of the widow, and her name,
come from reminiscences written by Thomas E. Lippincott and
published in the *Alton Telegraph*. Lippincott included his thoughts
about early Madison County in 47 letters for the Illinois Historical Society, at the request of W.G. Flagg, a local resident with an
interest in recording early Madison County history.[25]

After spending a short time in St. Louis, Lippincott arrived in
1818 at Milton, a small community along the Wood River not far
from the campsite. Then 21 years old, he opened a store in partnership with a man from St. Louis and remained at Milton until
1820 when he moved to Edwardsville. Milton, no longer existing,
contained two sawmills and a gristmill, a distillery and a tavern,
and the retail store. Lippincott wrote:

> There were two families residing between Milton and Alton;
> or more properly between Wood river and the Bates' farm.
> The first, near wood river was owned and occupied by a
> widow Meacham, who had been there during war time—
> the war of 1812—and as she told me, was visited by Indi-

ans on the same night I think on which the Wood river massacre occurred. The old lady was highly esteemed . . . she had two sons, men grown, and two or three daughters. . . . [26]

Lippincott also mentioned James Gillham, located in the American Bottom a few miles south of Milton. "He owned a fine farm and a ferry on the banks of the Mississippi opposite the mouth of the Missouri, most or at least much of which farm I believe has gone down the river, perhaps to the Gulf of Mexico."[27] Clark's notes and Ordway's journal references and the Lippincott memoir provide a nearly positive identification of the widow who had contact with men from Camp Dubois.

Lippincott had one more reference that connected with the Camp Dubois site. He wrote, "A year or so after I had moved to Edwardsville in 1820, I was called to marry my friend Ebenezer Huntington, to Margaret, the sister of Dr. Tiffin; the ceremony to be performed at his house in St. Mary's. I went and found a level plain at or near the mouth of Wood River on the lower [south side] with a two story framed house on it, in which Dr. Tiffin resided. That was St. Mary's."[28] This may be part of the campsite where Clark and company cleared timber for huts and shelter. Dr. Clayton Tiffin married Marie-Louise Jarrot, the oldest child of Nicholas Jarrot and they lived on the 400 acres once owned by her father and on which the party camped.

Also at issue among writers about the Camp Dubois site is the precise name of the Wood River and the appropriate name for the site. McDermott, a scholar of the region and particularly of the eighteenth century French in the Illinois country, concluded that early maps and documents identified it as *Riviere a Dubois*, or Dubois's River or Creek. Dubois, for whom it is named, may have been a resident as early as the mid-1700s. The name appeared on Soniat du Fossat's 1767 map of the area, nearly 40 years before the Corps arrived.[29]

McDermott called it the Dubois River rather than the Wood

River. For consistency, historians Osgood and Gary Moulton, editors of the field notes and journals, both referred to the site as
Camp Dubois. Clark acknowledged the stream as Wood River, or
Wood's River, but neither Lewis nor Clark used the camp names
in their writings.

Clark quickly began the chores of establishing a camp to serve
the Corps for five months. He organized the party for daily duties
such as hunting game, and preparing supplies, boats and provisions for the Missouri River journey. Meanwhile, Lewis, in St.
Louis and Cahokia, spent hours soaking up as much information
as cautious citizens would give him, and ordering supplies for the
trip. Lewis conferred often with John Hay deciding which individuals would most likely provide solid information for the captains. Hay acted as Lewis's interpreter on the visits.

At least one historian believes Lewis stayed with Hay in Cahokia
during this time.[30] During these conversations Hay and Lewis must
have had opportunities to talk of themselves and exchange personal information. While at Hay's house in Cahokia Lewis also
had access to the host's impressive library that offered a wide range
of current subjects and standard volumes. McDermott, who wrote
about Hay's library, called the Cahokian "a man of education and
taste."[31]

There is no telling how many volumes Hay's library had in
1803-04, but an estimate is possible from information filed after
his death. McDermott discovered in Hay's estate papers a list of
volumes that probably had its origin when Hay married and began rearing a family. Hay's library in 1843 contained volumes on
history, travels, memoirs, fiction, poetry, plays, and law. The au-
thors included Racine, Corneille, Shakespeare, Boileau, Irving and
poems by Freneau, gazetteers of Lewis Beck and John Mason Peck,
and Lavasseur's travels of Lafayette in America.

Familiar with diplomatic courtesies thanks to his time as
Jefferson's secretary in Washington, Lewis proceeded cautiously to
pry information from Spanish officials in St. Louis. With final action on the Louisiana Purchase pending, Lewis knew there would

be a reluctance to share vital statistics. Considering the long-standing Spanish distrust of Americans, Lewis might have expected unfriendly confrontations.

Antoine Soulard, surveyor general of Upper Louisiana, was one of Lewis's first targets for information among St. Louis officials. Lewis's keen sensitivity to cautions of the Spanish officials helped avoid any difficulties with Soulard. Instead of confrontation, Lewis and Soulard conducted a diplomatic dance that eventually benefited the American, and preserved the Frenchman's honor.

As the official with broad responsibility for land throughout Upper Louisiana, Soulard had information of potential great value to Lewis. A Frenchman with impeccable professional credentials, Soulard did his job well. American officials rewarded this competency after the Louisiana Purchase by retaining him in the surveyor's position.[32] A friendly recommendation from Lewis may have influenced the decision.

When they met, with Hay present as interpreter, Lewis told Soulard that the United States had no secrets, and assumed the same held true for Spain. Lewis later explained in a letter to Jefferson how he approached the situation, although unsure of Soulard's willingness to help. "I should feel no mortification at his withholding it [information] and I hoped he would feel no compunction in doing so, if he concieved his duty as an officer, or the policy of his government required it."[33]

Lewis began asking questions: Has the census of Upper Louisiana been taken recently? If so, what was the population? In this case Soulard was willing to share the information, but he reacted negatively when Lewis wanted to make a pen and ink copy in full view. According to Lewis, Soulard exclaimed, "Perhaps some person may come in." Soulard apologized for his reaction, begged forgiveness, and gave Lewis the information verbally. Soulard estimated the population at 10,000, including 2,000 slaves.[34] About two thirds of the remaining 8,000 were immigrants from the United States. Lewis, not allowed to write the number down, did his best to recall them for Jefferson. He had Hay for backup.

Lewis turned his queries to geography of the country and Soulard produced a map which the captain described as "imbracing a portion of the Mississippi, the Missouri from it's junction with this river to the mouth of the Osages, and the last named river in it's whole extent." Lewis asked for a copy of the map, but Soulard said while he had no objection, such a request had to be approved by various individuals. Soulard and Lewis later obtained the approvals and Lewis received a copy of the map.

The captain encountered hesitancy from other Spaniards as well, and concluded that they feared punishment or risked official displeasure if the commandant learned of indiscretions with an American. Lewis said the commandant "has produced a general dred of him among all classes of the people."[35] Lewis told Jefferson he expected officials would be more willing to talk after the United States officially gained control of Louisiana territory.

Nonetheless, Lewis called on a number of citizens and officials and asked questions or left a questionnaire he had prepared.[36] The document has never been recovered, nor any of the written responses, but Lewis repeated for Jefferson the kind of questions he had asked. He sought information about the quantity of lands granted to individuals, wealth of inhabitants, position and extent of settlements, state of agriculture and extent of improvements made on the lands that were inhabited.

Apparently Jefferson wanted that information to factor into an idea he had expressed to Lewis. Jefferson considered moving all Native Americans from U.S. lands east of the Mississippi to Louisiana territory, and in turn bringing all white inhabitants back east of the Mississippi. Lewis politely told Jefferson that this idea would not work primarily because of the differing attitudes of people in Louisiana. Apparently the president did not press the matter further.

Lewis found that information flowed more easily from traders and private individuals than through the official bureaucracy. He talked at length with Auguste Chouteau and his half-brother Jean Pierre, Gratiot, and fur trader Manuel Lisa. He left them questionnaires in hope of gaining valuable information from firsthand sources.

The only surviving confirmation of this approach to the traders and businessmen is a letter from Lewis to Auguste Chouteau written on January 4.[37] The document repeated the subject matter of geography and population, and added questions about dollars of trade brought into Upper Louisiana, amount of exports, mines and minerals, and animals, birds and fish of Louisiana. There is no record of Chouteau's reply.

The agenda of Lewis in St. Louis also included practical activities related to the upcoming journey. Recruiting for the crew continued. The captains needed voyagers—temporary helpers and not members of the permanent party—to push the boats against the current up the Missouri to the Mandan villages. Journals editor Moulton records the names or existence of 12 voyagers, many of them French residents of the Illinois country, who went as far as Mandan villages then returned to St. Louis. Lewis and Clark hired a number of these men in St. Louis.

Lewis also assumed partial responsibility for feeding the growing party at Camp Dubois. Fortunately, he had carte blanche from Jefferson to charge the costs of food and supplies to the military. Surviving receipts and payment vouchers give an idea of the items Lewis purchased.[38] They included charges for corn, flour, biscuits, salt, pork, candles, hog's lard, tools of all kinds, and bales of Indian goods. Lewis purchased them primarily from St. Louis sources, but also from Illinois country merchants.

Familiar names show up on the list of receipts and vouchers. Lewis authorized purchase of four horses from Charles Gratiot. He acknowledged receipt from Captain Stoddard for gunpowder weighing 75 pounds "for use of my command, bound to the western waters."[39] The boats that went up the Missouri were fortified with brass cannons mounted on swivels, and the crew carried large-gauge shotguns. They needed powder, too, for hunting on a daily basis. Through purchases in St. Louis, and at Camp Dubois, the captains gave the regional economy a boost.

The captains still had not completed the roster of permanent party upon arrival at the winter camp. At Fort Massac they had dispatched frontiersman George Drouillard to locate as many as eight soldiers who had been recruited from the Second Infantry Regiment at South West Point, Tennessee. Lewis and Clark hoped these men, with experience on the frontier, would complement the capabilities of those they recruited in Kentucky, at Massac, and Kaskaskia. Drouillard agreed to find the soldiers and bring them to Cahokia.

As expected, Drouillard and eight men arrived in Cahokia and met Lewis on December 16, four days after Clark arrived at Camp Dubois. In a letter the next day to Clark, Lewis offered his opinion of the recruits, and he did not think much of them. " . . . I am a little disappointed, in finding them not possessed of more of the requisite qualifications; there is not a hunter among them."[40] The Tennessee contingent included a blacksmith and a "house-joiner," which Lewis said might be of help at Camp Dubois.

In recognition of Drouillard's skills as an interpreter with Indians and his knowledge of the frontier, Lewis offered a civilian position with the permanent party. When they met at Fort Massac, Lewis had hired him temporarily and advanced $30 toward Drouillard's pay. In Cahokia he offered Drouillard $25 a month for as long as he remained with the party. Apparently Drouillard wanted to think it over and made no final deal in Cahokia. The group of nine left immediately for Camp Dubois.

Drouillard and the recruits arrived on the Wood River December 22, and Clark sized up the new men quickly in his notes for that date. "Drewyer & 8 men 2 horses arrive from Tennessee, those men are not such I was told was in readiness at Tennessee for this Comd &c &c . . ."[41] The captains agreed that the Tennessee commander sent soldiers of lesser quality. From the eight, Clark asked four to remain at Camp Dubois and sent the other four to Tennessee. One of those remaining, Corporal Richard Warfington, went as far as Fort Mandan, and commanded the group that returned to St. Louis in 1805. Privates Hugh Hall, Thomas P. Howard, and John Potts joined the permanent party.[42]

Clark wrote on Christmas day that Drouillard accepted Lewis's offer to accompany the party.[43] Drouillard left soon afterward for Fort Massac to settle personal affairs. As Lewis and Clark confirmed in their journals, Drouillard became one of the most valuable men on the journey. Seemingly, he did everything the captains asked, and became their most dependable hunter.

Meanwhile, Clark and sergeants in the party wasted no time in putting the men to work on Camp Dubois. The campsite, located in a heavily timbered area on the north end of the American Bottom, below the bluffs that marked the beginning of the Illinois prairie, needed immediate attention. The party had to fell trees before putting the huts together for shelter. Weather conditions complicated the task. The crew contended with wind blowing a gale off the nearby rivers, frequent snow and hail storms. If Clark wanted them to have a taste of what winter life on the trail to the Pacific might include, they got it at Camp Dubois.

On the way to Camp Dubois, Clark, Lewis, and non-commissioned officers had opportunities to talk and plan for the camp layout. Although they had not seen the site, Clark sketched possibilities for buildings. On a piece of paper just above Clark's notations for Saturday, December 17, he drew seven prospective camp layouts for huts and shelter.[44] Nothing in his notes or other documents indicates which of the choices he selected.

Clark's brief notes at the end of each day through the month of December tell of a relentless camp routine. There was one Clark entry that stated: "nothing remarkable to day." They hunted for game to supplement the corn and turnips, watched periodic boat traffic on the rivers, spoke with visiting and passing Indians, and worked on the huts except when it rained too hard, snowed or sleeted. Rarely did they allow the weather to delay work on shelter.

Shortly after arriving they cut a road of 2,490 yards, about one and a half miles, from the river to the prairie. They finished the first cabin, according to the notes, on December 16, and four

days later Clark said the men moved into their huts. Attention
then turned to hauling logs and constructing the captain's quarters. They started putting logs up for "my building" and Clark
paid a wagoner $3 for services. Later he noted the men's fatigue
from carrying logs, and then on December 30, a triumphant "I
move into my hut."[45]

Farmers from nearby found the party quickly after arrival and
brought food as gifts and for sale. Samuel Griffith made the first of
several appearances on December 16 to get acquainted and to bring
greetings. Griffith lived on a neck of land separating the Missouri
and Mississippi rivers, on the Louisiana side, long ago swept away
by the raging rivers. A week later Griffith brought a load of turnips, Clark said, "as a present to me." The next day Clark sent one
of the soldiers with Griffith to procure butter.

From the first day Indians visited Camp Dubois frequently.
One such occasion proved that in frontier times the world could
be small. Clark reported the visit of an unnamed Delaware Indian
chief whom he remembered from the signing of the Treaty of Fort
Greenville in Northwest Territory on August 3, 1795. Without
details from Clark, we can only imagine how they acknowledged
each other and what words they exchanged. The captain sent the
chief on his way with a bottle of whiskey.[46] On Christmas Day,
Indians joined the party for dinner. Clark's gift to the Indians: A
bottle of whiskey.

During the Christmas and New Year holiday period Clark
gave a first glimpse of disciplinary problems arising from excessive
drinking and fighting. Similar brief reports appeared several times
before they departed camp. Clark wrote of being awakened by a
gunshot, and learning that drinking and fighting occurred, but he
did not offer further comment. On New Year's Eve Clark prohib-
ited a man named Ramey from selling liquor to the soldiers. Among
the last words he wrote in 1803: "Colter Willard Leakens Hall &
Collins Drunk. Began to snow at Dark. . . ."[47]

12.

Counting the Days

The race was on. Around January 1, 1804, the crew finished the huts for soldiers and captains at Camp Dubois, concluding preliminaries to the winter camp. Many of the men who would make the first leg of the journey up the Missouri River had their orders and duties. Much needed to be done before the weather improved, such as repairing boats and wrapping and storing supplies and provisions. What could possibly go wrong?

As it turned out, nothing major went wrong. Many little things—less than cataclysmic, but important nonetheless—gave the captains moments of pause. In the end, the party remained at Camp Dubois a few weeks longer than originally planned in order to finish the work.

They strained to get everything done in the time allotted. Four and a half months from January 1 sounds like plenty of time to get the mission under way, but life in camp could not be devoted entirely to work on the voyage. Several men had camp duties such as cooking and posting guard. Snow, sleet, rain, blustery winds, thunderstorms, blowing sand and below zero temperatures restricted movement. The effects of weather distracted them, too. At one point during the coldest months, wind, snow and ice on the river caused the riverbanks to crumble. All able-bodied men scrambled to prevent damage to the boats. The first report by

Clark of riverbanks caving in occurred on January 6, after a siege of cold and wet weather. During the night Clark and some of the soldiers kept the boats upright as riverbanks began to crumble.[1] Ice jammed the Wood River. The next day Clark again expressed concern about the boats—a keelboat and two pirogues. Then the crisis eased as the weather broke and warmed.

Clark dutifully kept track of the weather in his field notes. He recorded the slightest variation, and consequences. "Verry cold," he wrote, and the words make you shiver. He kept track of ice floes on the Wood, Mississippi and Missouri rivers, and reported faithfully when the rivers rose, and when they receded. On January 17, the temperature dropped to eight degrees below zero. On January 22, it snowed five and three-quarters inches. He took the temperature in a corner of a building and found it was 20 degrees above zero.

While friendly neighbors in Illinois country brought a variety of goods to the camp as gifts and for trade—butter, corn, onions—the crew needed a daily requirement of meat that could be obtained only from hunting in the nearby woods. At least a handful of hunters went out every day and returned late in the afternoon. They procured an astonishing variety of meat: deer, wild hog, wildcat, muskrat, loon, badger, turkey, possum, squirrel, rabbit. The party ate well, but those who hunted could not be used for other duties.

Lack of discipline and dealing with it turned out to be the most time-consuming and serious distraction. While many in the party had experienced military time in garrison, a number had no military training and came to the Corps straight from life on the frontier. They did not welcome orders. These rough-cut men, used to living and acting independently, chafed at the regulation and military order. Keeping them under control for such a long time tested everyone.

There were the diversions you might expect in garrison, such as occasional drunkenness, rowdyism and fights, and disagreements that erupted into pushing, shoving and cursing. The captains expected the minor infractions. However, one minor incident often led to a more serious problem. The major discipline issues arose when crewmembers disobeyed orders and refused to perform as directed. Inattention and insubordination threatened camp security. The captains treated these incidents as serious matters, and devoted as much time as necessary to resolve them.

Clark's field notes for January and February reveal minor infractions more than anything serious. On January 1, he reported drunkenness among the soldiers, probably a carry-over from New Year's Eve.[2] Four days later he noted a fight between two soldiers. He ordered the men who had fought to build a hut for a woman who lived nearby. Clark mentioned only these incidents until late February. A breakdown in discipline accompanied by serious infractions occurred late that month with Clark in St. Louis and Lewis at Camp Dubois. We know of the crisis from two Detachment Orders Lewis issued to the soldiers.

On February 10, Lewis and Clark both left camp for business in St. Louis. Three days later Lewis returned to Dubois and stayed for about a week. Just before returning to St. Louis he issued the first Detachment Order addressing who would be left in charge in the absence of the two captains, and providing specific duties and expectations for the men. Lewis may have been in St. Louis more often than at Camp Dubois, but he did not shirk from his duties as a commander when required.

Lewis placed Sergeant Ordway in command during the captains' absence. Also he listed specific responsibilities for individual soldiers, including sawing plank, making sugar, and blacksmithing. Lewis ordered a ration of whiskey for those who performed their duties as expected. No one could leave camp without Ordway's permission, except those with hunting responsibilities.[3]

Lewis rejoined Clark in St. Louis on February 20. He returned to Dubois on February 29, and on March 3 issued as stern a Detachment Order as seen going or coming on the expedition. Upon arriving at camp Lewis found chaos among the troops, and the situation disturbed him. This is how Lewis expressed his displeasure:

> The Commanding officer feels himself mortified and disap-
> pointed at the disorderly conduct of Reubin Fields, in re-
> fusing to mount guard when in the due roteen of duty he
> was regularly warned; nor is he less surprised at the want of
> discretion in those who urged his oposition to the faithfull
> discharge of his duty, particularly Shields, whose sense of
> propryety he had every reason to believe would have in-
> duced him reather to have promoted good order. . . . [4]

The poor judgment of soldiers who openly defied Sergeant Ordway
appalled Lewis. He discovered that on at least one occasion four soldiers had left the base on the pretense of going hunting, only to head
directly to a nearby tavern. He cited them specifically in the order
and confined them to camp for ten days. The offending soldiers were
John Colter, John Boley, John Robertson and Peter Weiser.[5]

The case of John Shields received special attention when Clark
returned to camp after March 21. The captains ordered a trial for
Shields and several others accused of misconduct. They could have
been the other four mentioned by Lewis. Clark said the accused soldiers all asked forgiveness and promised to do better in the future.[6]
Exposure of that incident, and its resolution, did not bring a halt to
discipline troubles at the camp. On April 16 and again on May 2
Clark mentioned confinement of several soldiers for drunkenness. The
party could not leave Camp Dubois any too soon.

The captains learned to deal with discipline issues and other
command issues even though they only occasionally appeared in
camp together. Records indicate of the 141 days in Camp Dubois
after January 1, Lewis showed for 36, or about 25 per cent. Clark,
because his primary duty was to run the camp, spent 98 days at
Dubois or about 69 per cent, and about 43 days elsewhere. His
absences reflected an occasional respite from the duties of super-
vising the crew, welcoming Indian delegations, transacting business with the contractor who supplied goods, talking with visitors
from nearby farms and settlements, taking scientific readings, planning for the manning of boats on the journey, and evaluating sol-

diers in camp. Assessing soldiers' skills and demeanor took time but was especially critical in choosing men for the permanent party. Not everyone could make the whole journey.

Clark's health complicated performance of his duties. While there is no indication that Clark suffered from serious maladies at Camp Dubois, his notes attest to minor ailments on a number of occasions. Usually, he mentioned only being ill, or ill again, or still ill. From January 24 to January 27 he was sick. On January 31 he wrote, "head akes." He gave a similar report for February 3 to February 6. He never gave specifics, and he did not mention taking remedies. His health seemed to improve with the weather.

During the winter, when cold weather limited outdoor activity, Clark worked on two projects essential to the voyage. First, he assembled all maps available to the captains and prepared a composite.[7] This map was sent to Jefferson about the time of departure from Camp Dubois. Clark's field notes also reveal a sketch of the confluence of the rivers near the camp. Second, Clark used the maps and other data available about the Missouri River to produce an estimate of the miles they would travel to the Pacific Ocean, and the likely number of days required to reach the ocean and return.

Clark had no precise data for his estimates. The best information available covered the trip to the Mandan villages, and those guesses turned out to be the most accurate. Clark estimated a trip of 3,050 miles to the Pacific from Camp Dubois. The actual mileage was 3,958 miles.[8] Clark's estimate of 19 months for the round trip missed the mark. From Camp Dubois to the Pacific and back the expedition required 28 months and 10 days. There was no way to predict delays encountered at the Mandans, the slow-going over the Bitterroot mountains, and time spent at Fort Clatsop on the Pacific coast. For example, Clark believed the party would go beyond the Mandans for the first winter, but the Missouri River journey turned out to be more time-consuming than expected.

Clark and Lewis devoted substantial time in camp gathering valuable information about the journey ahead. They conferred with James Mackay, who lived in the St. Charles area. He spent almost two years on the middle-Missouri river and had maps and journals for the captains to use. The Whitesides visited frequently, and Nicholas Jarrot stopped on his way to trade with Indians at Prairie du Chien.

John Hay visited camp often, devoting most of the time to briefing the captains about the challenges ahead with Indians. Clark first noted a visit from Hay on January 30. He wrote, " . . . about Sun Set Capt Lewis arrived accompanied by Mr. J. Hay & Mr. Jo Hays of Kohokia. . . ."[9] The reference obviously was to both John Hay and his associate John Hays, sheriff of St. Clair County since 1798. Hays is often confused with John Hay because of the similar spelling of their names. Recent research, for example, has cast doubt on who was postmaster in Cahokia. The longtime assumption has been that Hay held the position, but there are enough unanswered questions to suggest that Hays might have been postmaster.

Hays worked as a youth for the Hudson's Bay Company in eastern and central Canada. After arriving in Cahokia in the early 1790s, he worked for the firm of Hay and Todd until it dissolved. He then began his own trading operation with activities at Prairie du Chien on the Mississippi.[10] Clark welcomed Hays to the campsite because of his experience with Indians and knowledge of the fur trade in the Red River country. On February 1, Clark wrote that he had ridden a horse belonging to Hays for six miles, with no further information. On February 2, Clark saw them off to Cahokia.

Through the winter Clark mixed pleasure with the work, breaking away periodically for exploration of the camp vicinity. One day in January he rode south a few miles to the northwest edge of Cahokia mounds near present-day Mitchell.[11] The northern group of mounds does not exist today because of growth and development that occurred before efforts were made to preserve the historic sites. When Clark returned before sunset he found his feet had frozen to his shoes, which prompted him to warn others of the frostbite danger.

Other diversions from labors at camp included social events in St. Louis and Cahokia. The captains were in demand in St. Louis for dinners and parties, and because Lewis visited there more often, he had a brisk social life. Clark went for special occasions. On February 8 Clark wrote that Hay sent a messenger from Cahokia with letters and an invitation to two balls in St. Louis.[12] Clark and Lewis left Dubois two days afterward for St. Louis, presumably to conduct business and attend the parties. Lewis missed the parties, however, as he returned to Dubois, while Clark remained in St. Louis.

Another trip to St. Louis occurred April 7 when the captains left Dubois for St. Louis at 7 a.m. in a canoe, accompanied by York, Clark's slave, and one other person. Clark wrote that they arrived about 10:30 a.m. Later in the day they "Dressed & Dined with Capt Stoddard & about 50 Gentlemen, A Ball succeeded, which lasted untill 9 oClock on Sunday."[13] Such a sizable crowd meant it must have been an official function that brought guests from the town and beyond. This may have been the event which Captain Stoddard held to repay the kindness extended during the transfer of Louisiana to the United States and his tenure as commandant for the United States. Clark took advantage of the respite and remained in St. Louis several days to rest and conduct business.

Those were minor events compared to the principal ceremonial occasion of the year, or for any year, held in March. Lewis and Clark both appeared for two days, along with dignitaries from across the region for the St. Louis version of the Louisiana Purchase transfer. Lewis had official duty as President Jefferson's personal representative, but Clark attended just for the occasion. Actually, he had been in St. Louis a number of days, conferring with fur trader Manuel Lisa, hiring voyagers for the trip to the Mandans, and conducting miscellaneous business.

The official transfer of Louisiana occurred in New Orleans on December 20. For diplomatic considerations President Jefferson ordered a separate surrender of Upper Louisiana be made in St. Louis. The circumstances of French ownership, and Spanish occupation of St. Louis, required special consideration to preserve the pride of French residents. Responsibility for conducting a sensitive event fell to Captain Stoddard, who had been in St. Louis for

several weeks preparing to take over as commissioner and temporary military and civil leader of the vast Upper Louisiana region.[14]
In a short time Stoddard demonstrated a keen diplomatic sense in
dealings with Spanish officials and French citizens. In this delicate
position, Stoddard became an important contact for the captains
among the leaders of St. Louis.

In one of the more unusual aspects of the transfer in St. Louis,
Stoddard fulfilled two important roles. After the transfer in New
Orleans the French had no officials in Upper Louisiana. Consequently Pedro Clemente Laussat, commissioner of the French Re-
public, appointed Stoddard as agent for France, in addition to his
official role for the United States.[15] At Government House in St.
Louis on March 9 everyone gathered for the first of two official
events. Stoddard scheduled the second for the following day. Carlos
Dehault Delassus, Spanish commandant in St. Louis, transferred
possession of Upper Louisiana to Stoddard, who represented France.
Emotions flowed among the citizens of St. Louis, almost all of
whom were French and had not supported the transfer.[16]

Being especially considerate of these feelings, Charles Gratiot
took matters into his own hands, presumably with the approval of
Stoddard. Most of the inhabitants of St. Louis did not understand
English, so Gratiot translated Stoddard's speech in French. Gratiot
also translated in French and English the words spoken by Governor Delassus.[17]

After the Spanish flag was struck, Delassus presented it to
Stoddard, who then hoisted the French Tricolor over St. Louis for
one final 24-hour period. The French citizens cheered and cried.
The next day, when officials lowered the French flag and raised the
American flag, Gratiot called for a cheer from the French crowd.
One written report called it "a little half-hearted."[18] Lewis, Delassus,
Stoddard, Soulard and Gratiot signed final cession papers record-
ing the transfer to the United States.

After that, no more official or unofficial barriers remained for
the Corps of Discovery to enter Upper Louisiana on its way to the
Pacific. Lewis and Clark remained in St. Louis for several days after

the ceremony, conducting business and making a tour of Spanish military installations in the area with Stoddard. After a diversion to St. Charles with Lewis, Pierre Chouteau and Gratiot to stop Kickapoo Indians from going to war against the Osages, Clark returned to Dubois on March 21.[19] During this side trip, it is possible that Lewis and Clark encountered James Mackay, who commanded a military post for the Spanish government in the vicinity. Mackay mobilized his post for troubles with the Osages. Mackay's journey up the Missouri River in 1795-97 became a major source of information for the captains. Back at Camp Dubois the pace quickened toward the day of departure. A week later, Clark's field notes sounded the charge: "All hands at work prepareing for the voyage up the Missourie."

Clark's notes for the next month reveal the priority of business, and record a number of distractions. He commented on preparation of the keelboat and pirogues, which required a major commitment of manpower at camp. Those with special skills, such as blacksmithing and carpentering, worked on this project and modified the keelboat interior for better loading, defense and protection of supplies. Appleman of the National Park Service, described a change designed to provide relief from the elements:

> Another substantive modification was erection over the hold of three removable ridgepoles, resting on center supports that were forked at the top. These poles held up the center of an awning that was lashed to the sides of the boat. A similar ridgepole awning also apparently covered the cabin deck.[20]

They made few changes in the pirogues, but provided all boats with armament. Appleman explains:

> On the bow of the large boat a small cannon was mounted on a swivel so it could be turned and fired in any direction . . . Representing the expedition's heaviest armament

and at the time the largest weapon ever taken up the Missouri, it was capable of delivering a deadly discharge at close
range and would be valuable for persuasion or defense among
the natives. Two smaller swivel guns, probably blunderbusses, were mounted on the stern of the keelboat and one
each on the two pirogues . . .

The handling and storage of provisions and goods on the boats
required concentrations of crew time. Clark recorded full days of
packing and storing goods for the journey, including flour, corn,
whiskey and pork.[21] The agent for a military contractor who provided goods, Major Nathan Rumsey, appeared frequently, signaling the shortage of time remaining for packing the boats. During
this period Clark made two trips totaling eight days to St. Louis
on business and pleasure.

With a few weeks remaining, decision time arrived for naming
the permanent party, and also determining those who would go
only as far as the Mandan villages, then return to St. Louis. During the first three months at Camp Dubois the captains evaluated
each individual's capabilities and conferred on who should go to
the Pacific Ocean. The captains ended speculation among the troops
with a detachment order dated April 1, that listed the party members.[22] They organized the crew into three squads of eight men
each and named Sergeant Nathaniel Pryor, Sergeant Charles Floyd
and Sergeant John Ordway as squad leaders. The captains designated a fourth group headed by Corporal Richard Warfington for
the trip only as far as the Mandan villages.

The order listed the 24 permanent party members as William
E. Bratten, John Colter, John Collins, Reubin Field, Joseph Field,
Charles Floyd, Patrick Gass, George Gibson, Silas Goodrich, Tho-
mas P. Howard, Hugh Hall, Hugh McNeal, John Ordway,
Nathaniel Hale Pryor, John Potts, Moses B. Reed, George Shan-
non, John Shields, John B. Thompson, Richard Winser, William
Werner, Peter M. Weiser, Joseph Whitehouse, and Alexander
Hamilton Willard.

Those assigned to return from the Mandan villages were John Boley, John Dame, Thomas Proctor Howard, John Newman, John Robertson, Ebenezer Tuttle, Isaac White, and Richard Warfington, the non-commissioned officer in charge.

Changes in the roster continued during the journey to the Mandan villages, and during the winter of 1804-05. Speculation remains as to the exact number and names of the party that went to the Mandans. For example, Newman was tried and convicted of "mutinous expression" in October, 1804, and expelled from the party. Moses Reed was scratched after deserting and being convicted in a trial. Robert Frazer, whose name appears in later documents, was a substitute. George Drouillard, a civilian, did not appear on the April list, and neither did York. Nevertheless, the list provides a good idea of those who went to the Pacific and returned, and that the permanent party numbered about 30, including the captains. The best guess about the number of men that headed to the Mandans in May is approximately 50, including temporary voyagers.[23]

Sergeant Ordway offered a number for the party in a letter to his parents in New Hampshire on April 8. He said the permanent party consisted of 25 men and that he was "so happy to be one of them." Ordway said the journey would begin in 10 days—about April 18—and would require most of two years. His mention of a departure date in mid-April missed the mark by almost a month, but reflected the pressure to get under way and the additional work that needed to be done. Ordway's estimate of time for the entire trip compares favorably with Clark's. Ordway said he would receive a "great Reward" when the expedition returned.[24]

Intensity of efforts in camp increased markedly during April. As the departure date for the Corps approached, preparations for the journey occupied everyone in camp. All the items the captains and party had accumulated over nearly four months had to be packed and loaded. Hay arrived from Cahokia on April 26 to help the crew pack goods to be used as gifts with Indians. He remained in camp until May 2, when he returned to Cahokia.

Hay's appearance at this critical juncture is not surprising. Clark and his crew listened to Hay and learned. Hay drew on all those years of watching his father and listening to him tell of preparing gifts for the Indians. He remembered going back and forth from upper Michigan to the Assiniboine and Souris river country to trade with the Indians. Hay learned about trade with Indians from the experts: His father, Andrew Todd, Charles Gratiot and Jacques Clamorgan. These experiences made Hay as close to an expert himself in preparing for encounters with the Otos, Poncas, Omahas, Mandans and Arikaras. Ronda describes how Hay packaged trade goods, medals, flags, fancy dress uniforms, and all the presents brought from Philadelphia:

> As an experienced trader he knew the finer points of packaging and merchandising. It was probably Hay who suggested putting a variety of gifts into bags protected by waterproof fabric. Those bags were first divided into two general groups, one for the Indians on the river up to the Mandans and a second set for "foreign nations." All told, there were to be twenty-one bags of Indian goods . . . Knowing the great power of Omaha leaders like the late Chief Blackbird, they set aside a separate part of one bag for the leading Omaha chief.[25]

Why didn't Hay just pack up and go with the captains? At least as far as the Mandans? First, there is no reason to believe that Hay wanted to join the expedition for the Pacific or that the captains asked him to go. With a wife and children in Cahokia, and holding important government positions, Hay was not in the picture as a prospective voyager. Hay's days as a frontiersman were a decade old, and his body was older, too. However, with intimate details of Lewis's and Clark's plans and knowledge of their anxieties and hopes, Hay must have wondered why this opportunity didn't come along 10 years earlier before he had settled down to family life.

Three other documents regarding Hay are part of the Lewis and Clark record. One reflects the high regard Lewis held for the Illinoisan; a second by Lewis mentioned a recommendation by Hay; and a third, written by Hay, provided the captains with detailed information about the Red River region. They complete the written record about Hay and the expedition during the winter of 1803-04.

Donald Jackson, who assembled the documents of Lewis and Clark, also found records of four letters written by Lewis to Jefferson from December 28 to March 26 in the president's letter index, none of which has survived.[26] In the same time period Lewis wrote a number of letters to Secretary of War Henry Dearborn which are part of the Department of War inventory. Among those letters was one written by Lewis on April 4, 1804, regarding a recommendation of John Hay for a subagency with Indians. There is no record of any action by the secretary.

In April, no specific date given, Clark wrote a "Memorandum of Artecles which may be wanting" to Lewis.[27] The memo mentioned red lead and oil paints for lockers on the decks of the boats, nails for hinges, ribbon, and personnel issues. Midway in the memo, Clark wrote, "I can't find Hair Pipes purchased of Mr. Chouteau. Mr. Hays says they are necessary." "Hair pipe" was a term used for a variety of tubular beads 1.5 or more inches in length and used by Indians of the Plains. This provides further evidence of Hay's expertise in dealing with Indians.

Various documents that are vital parts of the Lewis and Clark record have surfaced over the years, found among papers of individuals close to the captains and wrapped in anonymous looking packages. Long after the expedition and publication of the journals researchers found a single loose sheet of paper that Hay probably gave to Lewis during the winter of 1803-04.

Clark wrote at the top of the sheet, "The names of the Forts or British Trading Establishments on the Ossiniboin."[28] Hay described a trip down the Red River into southern Manitoba (the river flows north) and listed streams that are tributaries of the Red (bordering North Dakota and Minnesota). The captains took the sheet with them and Clark wrote his own notes on the paper, probably at Fort Mandan.

From these sources, and others, Lewis and Clark assembled an extraordinary amount of information before leaving Camp Dubois. They especially had learned more about the Missouri River as far as the Mandan Villages. But the captains knew from experience that answers to their questions and those of Thomas Jefferson would be known only when the journey ended.

Maybe the worst news for Lewis and Clark at a personal level occurred in May when Lewis received a letter from Secretary of War Dearborn denying the request to make Clark a captain in the army. Dearborn wrote, "The peculiar situation, circumstances and organisation of the Corps of Engineers is such as would render the appointment of Mr. Clark a Captain in that Corps improper—and consequently no appointment above that of a Lieutenant in the Corps of Artillerists could with propriety be given him which appointment he has recd. and his Commission is herewith enclosed."[29]

For Lewis this came close to official betrayal. Jefferson promised that Lewis and Clark each would have the rank of captain, with equal pay and benefits. Had Clark been any less a loyalist to Lewis and the mission, the whole matter might have erupted in a bitter public outcry. Clark suppressed his disappointment, and the two commanders went on with their duties.

Lewis sent the commission in a letter to Clark on May 6, with his own promise. "I think it will be best to let none of our party or any other persons know any thing about the grade, you will observe that the grade has no effect upon your compensation, which by G____d, shall be equal to my own."[30] It is part of Lewis and Clark Expedition legend that the two referred to each other as "captain" and never revealed Clark's actual rank to members of the crew.

The final chapter of the episode occurred when Clark returned from the journey and quietly turned in his commission without comment. Questioned later by Nicholas Biddle, who edited and published the captains' journals, Clark said, "I did not think myself very well treated. . . ."[31] Speculation continues as to why Lewis's request was denied, and why he apparently did not appeal. Others surmise Jefferson may have wanted one person in command.

When May arrived the Corps of Discovery had just two weeks remaining in the Illinois country. Counting from the time when the party stopped at Kaskaskia on November 28, Lewis, Clark and the crew had spent almost six months in settlements of the Illinois country preparing for the moment when they could leave on the Missouri River. The final two weeks in the Illinois country had begun.

Aware that the expedition force soon would leave the Illinois country, citizens who had spent time with the soldiers since December visited the camp on several occasions.[32] On May 6 Illinois visitors engaged some of the soldiers in a shooting accuracy game. Clark wrote, "In Camp Shooting with the party all git beet and lose their money."

The comings, goings and events as recorded briefly by Clark seemed almost to down-play the importance of the work being done. John Hay spent his final time at Dubois and left for Cahokia. Several soldiers were found drunk. Clark sent maps to St. Louis. Indians visited the camp. Clark sent maps to Lewis in St. Louis. He wasted no time with elaborate descriptions or explanations.

Work was done on the keelboat in advance of May 7, when loading began. A day later the crew loaded the keelboat and pirogues, and manned the boat with 20 oars for a trial excursion up the Mississippi a few miles. As days passed, the crew adjusted the load on the keelboat and Clark ordered every man carrying muskets to have 100 balls for the rifles and two pounds of buckshot.

The pace quickened. Manuel Lisa, one of the first fur traders on the Missouri after return of Lewis and Clark in 1806, arrived from St. Louis for an unexplained visit. Signaling the final days in camp, the party moved from the buildings into tents. Finally, a day before departure Clark reported to Lewis: "All in health and readiness to Set out. Boats and every thing Complete, with the necessary Stores of provisions & such articles of merchendize as we thought ourselves autherised to precure. . . ."[33]

Clark made a final entry in the Camp Dubois field notes on May 14: "A Cloudy morning fixing for a Start Some provisions on examination is found to be wet rain at 9 oClock Many of the Neighbours Came from the Countrey Mail and feeMail rained the greater part of the day, I set out at 4 oClock to the head of the first Island in the Missourie 6 Miles and incamped, on the Island rained. . . ."[34]

13.

Unlocking the Missouri

Before leaving on the expedition Lewis and Clark knew little about specific explorations of the Missouri River, and had no documents from the earliest journeys on the river. While in the Illinois country the captains obtained written accounts of two expeditions, and maps that provided accurate and precise details up to the Mandan Indian villages.

While the captains were on the Ohio River heading to the Illinois country, President Jefferson wrote a letter to Lewis on November 16, 1803, providing the first documentary evidence of an exploration of the Missouri. In the letter, which arrived long after the party reached the Illinois country, Jefferson said, "I inclose you . . . some information collected by myself from Truteau's journal in MS. all of which may be useful to you. . . ." Jefferson attached his extracts of the Jean Baptiste Truteau journal containing mostly numbers and names of Indian tribes encountered by the explorer, and information about conditions on the Missouri.[1]

After the captains arrived at Camp Dubois and had opportunities to talk with Illinoisans, they learned of more extensive travels on the river than those of Truteau. Initially the Truteau journal had valuable information, but it took second place quickly when Lewis and Clark obtained the records of James Mackay and John Thomas Evans, who followed Truteau on the Missouri. The Mackay and Evans documents eventually became the primary river travel guide for Lewis and Clark.[2]

Ten years before Lewis and Clark started up the Missouri River one of the first recorded explorations of the river's lower region, headed by Truteau, began from St. Louis. Others before him had struck out for the upper Missouri to trap and hunt, but Truteau's venture marked one of the first excursions financed by a company determined to reach the Pacific Ocean.[3]

In the early 1790s Spanish officials of Upper Louisiana wanted desperately to stop the British advance into the Upper Missouri (North Dakota and Montana) fur trade. Spain also wanted to extend its claims to the Pacific coast, which it called the "south sea." This official desire to expand brought together individuals already familiar to this story: Jacques Clamorgan, Andrew Todd, and Spanish leaders in St. Louis. The instrument for financing excursions to the Pacific was the Missouri Company.

Clamorgan, Todd and the Spanish agreed on three explorations of the Missouri, leading to a final push for the Pacific.[4] They found their first adventurer teaching school in St. Louis. Jean Baptiste Truteau, born in Montreal in 1748, came to St. Louis at age 26, where he may have been one of the first teachers in the new town. In order to earn extra money Truteau took short trips to trade with nearby Indians.[5] These brief journeys constituted his experience in the wilderness.

Funded and equipped by the Missouri Company, Truteau and eight men in a pirogue left St. Louis on June 7, 1794, with the stated objective of reaching the Mandan Indian villages by winter. Operating under a two-year contract with the Missouri Company, Truteau had orders to build a fort, establish an agency and remain until relieved. His employers insisted that he keep a daily journal, and ordered him to engage with the Mandans and tell them they must trade only with agents of the Spanish.[6] They wanted Truteau to explore, to observe, to deliver messages, and to spy on the British.

The leader's inexperience and an inadequate number of men handicapped the expedition from the outset. Along the Missouri the party encountered aggressive Indians who cleaned them out of goods they brought along for appeasement. Indian problems and a difficult trip up river undermined the timetable for arrival at the Mandan villages. For shelter that first winter Truteau built a camp in modern day Charles Mix County, South Dakota, a little above and opposite the site that later became Fort Randall. Truteau called the camp "Ponca House."[7]

In the spring of 1795 Truteau resumed the journey, stopping this time with the Arikara Indians, still south of the Mandans. A few members of the crew took their lone pirogue to transport furs to St. Louis, leaving the main party stranded. Mindful of a second Missouri Company exploration scheduled to begin that spring, Truteau decided to wait for relief. The party stayed through 1795 without a friendly face appearing, as the second exploration bogged down below the Arikara Indian camp. That group gave up and returned to St. Louis.[8] A third exploration headed by Mackay and his Welsh associate Evans—about whom we will hear more—also started up the Missouri in 1795. Strangely, they did not find Truteau either.

Confused and beaten, Truteau returned by river transportation to St. Louis by the summer of 1796, the end of his two-year contract. His journey cost the Missouri Company a large sum and produced unimpressive results. Truteau returned to teach in St. Louis. He lived in the vicinity when Lewis and Clark visited, but there is no record of conversations among the three. The teacher-explorer died in 1827.

Historians have mixed feelings about the value of Truteau's journals. Nasatir and McDermott wrote that Truteau's journals contained valuable information on geography and some accurate reports from Indians regarding the Yellowstone River country.[9] Ronda, who has written extensively of Lewis and Clark's involvement with Indians, minimized the value of Truteau's journal extracts. He says the notes contain erroneous information and failed to explain the complex relations among Indian groups on the Missouri.[10]

Information from Truteau's journey pales when compared to

data from the explorations of Mackay and Evans. They, too, kept journals, but also drew maps that provided the most complete, up-to-date information for the captains. Their experiences took them well beyond the last stop by Truteau, providing new experiences on which to draw. The two men produced by far the most valuable information about the geography and Indians up to the Mandan villages, and on to the sources of the Missouri. Their records clarified fragments of information and speculation previously provided to the captains.[11]

It is believed Mackay was born in 1759 in Arrichliney, parish of Kildonan, County of Sutherland, in northeastern Scotland. His Scottish ancestors included Irish royalty, descendants of the ancient "race of O'Connor." He migrated to North America about 1776, landing in Canada.[12] Then younger than 20, Mackay like so many who drifted to Montreal, found his way into the fur trade. He made voyages and journeys for English merchants to central Canada in 1784, 1786, 1787, and 1788.

There is speculation that Mackay visited the Mandan villages in 1787. If so he was one of the earliest white men to encounter the Indians who befriended Lewis and Clark twice on their journey. This familiarity with geography and trade on the Red River, the Assiniboine River, and with the Mandans gave Mackay a common bond with John Hay, who made similar trips late in the 1780s and early 1790s. Mackay probably came to the Illinois country about the same time as Hay in 1793.

Within two years of Mackay's arrival in the area controlled by the Spanish near St. Louis, the Missouri Company chose Mackay to lead an exploration of the Missouri River and complete the journey of Truteau, then stranded in the vicinity of the South Dakota-Nebraska border. It is easy to understand why Clamorgan and the Spanish liked the Scot. Mackay's familiarity with the Mandan country and his knowledge of British trade provided an ideal background to help the Spanish with its strategy to oust the English from the Upper Missouri.

The Missouri Company engaged Mackay as "principal explorer

and director of the Company's affairs in the Indian country," with orders to build forts wherever he thought they should be constructed, and to protect Spanish trade from the British. Mackay explained the mission: "In 1795 authorized by Mr. Zenon Trudeau Lieut. Govr. Of the Illinois by the River Missouri by the Mississippi. The object of this Voyage was to open a commerce with those distant and Unknown Nations in the upper parts of the Missouri and to discover all the unknown parts of his Catholic Majesty's Dominions through that continent as far as the Pacific Ocean."[13]

The Missouri Company learned a lesson about crew size from the Truteau experiment, and this time provided Mackay with ample manpower. Accompanied by 33 men in four pirogues, Mackay and Evans left St. Louis at the end of August, 1795.[14] For two months the party labored to the mouth of the Platte River in present-day Nebraska where Mackay built a house for people he left behind with the Oto Indians. As winter neared, the party slowly moved upriver to a village of the Omaha Indians. Mackay built Fort Charles, located about six miles below present-day Omandi, Nebraska, and stayed through the winter.[15] He made friends with the Omahas, at a considerable cost. He used up almost all the gifts and presents and had to wait for reinforcements and fresh supplies from St. Louis.

Mackay's schedule having unraveled, he sent Evans up the Missouri to rendezvous with Truteau. Evans encountered Indian trouble and returned to Fort Charles without having met Truteau's party. In the spring of 1796, Evans again headed up the Missouri and visited the Arikara and Mandan Indians. Near the Mandan villages he chased out British traders and took possession of their fort. This is believed to be as far up the Missouri River as either Mackay or Evans progressed.[16]

Mackay's activities during 1796 and 1797 are difficult to trace, although he did travel west on tributaries of the Missouri in Nebraska territory. At some point in those months Evans and Mackay drew maps and completed their journals.[17] They returned to St. Louis by May, 1797, when the Spanish treated Mackay as a hero.

In spite of the failure to push on to the Pacific Ocean, Mackay and Evans returned with new information, and had made their presence known to the British.

To show their appreciation, Spanish officials in New Orleans appointed Mackay captain of militia and commandant of San Andre del Misuri in 1798, an establishment not far from the mouth of the Missouri in the vicinity of St. Charles which Mackay chose. Evans received compensation from the Spanish, but no immediate official position. He died in 1798. The Spanish gave Mackay land and opportunities to engage in Indian trade, all to repay him for the dangers and deprivations of life on the Missouri. Nasatir describes Mackay's standing with the Spanish in these words: "Mackay was uniformly characterized by the officials of Spanish Louisiana as a man of ability, intelligence . . . loyalty and honesty, a man of knowledge, zealous and punctual," although he failed to meet Spanish objectives for the expedition.[18]

More important to his future on American soil after the Louisiana Purchase, Mackay became a friend of Antoine Soulard, surveyor general of Upper Louisiana. After the transfer of Louisiana to the United States, Soulard selected Mackay as a deputy surveyor. Also, Spanish officials recommended Mackay to Captain Stoddard as a man of good qualities who read and wrote Spanish. Mackay had solid political standing when the U.S. officially took over Louisiana from the French. Temporary Louisiana Territory Governor Harrison appointed him a judge of the Court of Quarter Sessions.[19]

The exact time when Lewis and Clark encountered Mackay personally is difficult to determine. Given the proximity of St. Charles to Camp Dubois, Mackay could have visited Clark several times during 1804. However, Clark records only one visit by Mackay and provides little information about their discussions. In his notes of January 10, Clark wrote: "Cap. Mackey has Just returned from Surveying of some lands up the Missouras, which has been lately granted he says 'a boutifull Countrey presents it self on the route he went & returned. . . .'"[20]

Lewis, and probably Clark, knew of the journey of Mackay

and Evans and the existence of journals and maps several weeks earlier. In Lewis's letter to Jefferson of December 28, he wrote, "... I have also obtained Ivins's and Mac Kay's journal up the Missouri, it is in French & is at present in the hands of Mr. Hay, who has promised to translate it for me; I am also promised by Mr. Hay a copy of his journal from Michilimackinack to the Assinaboin river in the north...."[21] The letters of Harrison, Jefferson and Lewis suggest that Hay and Mackay knew each other prior to the arrival of Lewis and Clark, and Hay brought the explorer into direct contact with the captains. He assisted Lewis as well with a translation of the Mackay-Evans journal.

The Mackay and Evans maps are viewed as particularly important to Lewis and Clark because of their role in the total picture of maps available to the captains, and maps they drew before leaving the Illinois country.[22] Beginning with the earliest days of planning in Washington, Jefferson and Lewis had the latest maps to study. However, historians question the validity of the early maps, and place credibility on the maps discovered and copied after arriving in the Illinois country.

While the Mackay-Evans material had flaws, it provided Lewis and Clark with the best map information available. At the same time, Lewis and Clark obtained valuable maps from Antoine Soulard, whose job in St. Louis was to survey land in Upper Louisiana. Soulard entered the picture with Lewis in December. In the letter from Lewis to Jefferson on December 28, the captain tells of his conversations in St. Louis early in December and mentions receiving three maps. This is how Lewis described them:

"I have obtained three maps; one of the Osages river ... a general map of the Uper Louisiana, and a map of the Missouri river, from it's mouth to the Mandane nation...."[23] The map of the Osage River was from Soulard, and is believed to have been a copy that he gave to Lewis. The original map never has been found. The general map presumably came from Soulard, and the map of Upper Louisiana, judging from its description, could only have been a copy of a Mackay map received by Lewis and Clark, historians believe.

Two maps of the Missouri originated from the Mackay-Evans journey, one from each of the two explorers.[24] The map believed drawn by Mackay covers the journey to Fort Charles, and not much further. The second map was produced by Evans on seven sheets, six of which covered the route to the Mandan-Hidatsa villages. The seventh sheet is a speculative document that shows a route to the Rocky Mountains.[25] Evans's document has been lauded by historians because of information it provided beyond the confluence of the Yellowstone and Missouri rivers.[26] Since neither man went that far, Evans presumably obtained the information from Indians he visited. Mackay also may have used data from Evans for his map, which has made it difficult to determine exactly which of the two explorers did what work. Regardless of authorship, for the first time Lewis and Clark had a depiction of the area west of the Mandans (in North Dakota and Montana), supplemented by journals.

While the maps provided accurate geographical information about the river to the Mandans, both men made mistakes in estimating distances. Mackay placed the Mandan villages 400 miles beyond their exact location from St. Louis, and Evans's map showed the Mandans 300 miles further than the exact location of the villages. Although distances as recorded by Mackay and Evans turned out to be off the mark, they provided an improvement in accuracy over earlier maps available to Lewis in Washington. Bombarded as they were by rumors and gossip among traders and voyagers about the Missouri, Lewis and Clark appreciated the Mackay-Evans documents for their specific information, validated in conversations with Soulard and Hay.

There is little doubt that Lewis and Clark used the Mackay and Evans material as they moved up the Missouri. Clark's journal from Camp Dubois to the Mandans includes frequent references to Mackay's map and journals. A copy of the Evans map has frequent notations in Clark's handwriting.[27]

Mackay and Evans's journals supplemented their maps and

influenced the captains' impression of what they might encounter on the Missouri. How Lewis and Clark obtained the maps is important when considering the hands through which they passed and the connections to prime players in the drama. Soulard, Jefferson, Harrison and Hay all make appearances in the Mackay-Evans map story.

The first mention of the Mackay and Evans maps and journals and Mackay's supplemental table of distances occurred in a letter from Harrison written in Vincennes on November 13, 1803, to his friend Clark. At that time Lewis and Clark had just started their journey up the Mississippi to the Illinois country. Not knowing exactly when or where Clark would receive his letter, Harrison had the letter addressed to "Captain William Clark or Captain Meriwether Lewis on their way up the Mississippi supposed to be at Cahokia." The letter's endorsement stated, "Govr. Harrison has sent by the post rider a map for Captn. Clark which Dr. [George] Fisher will be so obliging as to forward to Cahokia with this letter."[28] The letter said in its entirety:

> The map mentioned in your letter of the 5th Instant has been taken from me by Mr. Jones who claimed it as the property of Mr. Hay of Cahokia but as it was still in the possession of Mr. Jones I have had it copied & now send it to you by the Post rider—whom I have been obliged to detain for that purpose. I hope it will arrive safe. Your offer to let me hear from you occasionally I accept with a great deal of pleasure—& I beg of you to let me Know from Cahokia whether I can do any thing for you in yr. absence. The mail of last night brought us the information that the Senate had advised the ratification of the French Treaty 24. To 7. There were 8 of the opposition present but Dayton voted with the Majority. Give my respects to Captn. Lewis & ask him to spend a few days with me on his return.[29]

The assumption is that Harrison sent Clark a copy of the

Mackay map made in 1797 showing the Missouri River route from the Mississippi to the Mandans. "Mr. Jones" referred to John Rice Jones, then postmaster in Vincennes. Harrison's mention of Hay suggests the Cahokian had obtained the map directly from Mackay, or from Soulard in St. Louis and sent it to Harrison at territorial headquarters. If the date referred to by Harrison is November 5, Clark wrote the governor before the captains left Clarksville, Indiana, on the Ohio River. At that stage Clark had no knowledge of the Mackay map, but probably wrote Harrison asking for anything the governor might have or find.

A letter from Harrison to President Jefferson on November 26 introduces the Evans map. Harrison wrote:

> The Governor of the Indiana Territory presents his respect-
> ful compliments to the President of the United States and
> requests his acceptance of the enclosed map which is a Copy
> of the manuscript map of Mr. Evans who ascended the
> Missouri River by order of the Spanish Government much
> further than any other person.[30]

The Evans map is not mentioned again until Jefferson's letter to Lewis on January 13, 1804. Jefferson wrote, in part, "I now inclose you a map of the Missouri as far as the Mandans, 12. or 1500. miles I presume above it's mouth. It is said to be very accurate, having been done by a Mr. Evans by order of the Spanish government. . . ."[31] Jefferson referred to the Evans map again in a letter to Lewis on January 22. By that time Lewis had all the available maps in hand.

The Evans journal and perhaps the map had been circulated among Illinoisans since 1797. Moses Austin kept extensive notes of his journey that year to the Illinois country, including the time he stayed at Whiteside Station in St. Clair County. Austin enjoyed the hospitality of William Whiteside, and received advice about traveling in the region. "I found Mr. Whiteside to be in possion of some information respecting the country which he gave me freely, he also informed me that he had Sundry letters from a Mr. Evens 2500 miles up the Missouri. . . ."[32] Austin copied an extract which he included in the notes. In the excerpt Evans tells of experiences with the Omaha Indians on the Missouri, and of being driven back by less friendly Indians to that location when he tried to advance northward on the river.

The value of maps and journals belonging to Mackay and Evans is endorsed by every historian who has spent time with the material and attempted to sort out authorship. The fact remains that Lewis and Clark put the explorers' material together with everything they accumulated during the six months in the Illinois country, and decided on their own what to use and what to discard. The Spanish explorations clearly were highly regarded by the captains.

Nasatir puts the efforts of Spanish exploration—principally Truteau, Mackay and Evans—in perspective for students of Lewis and Clark:

> Although the task of reaching the Pacific Ocean via the Missouri, attempted so enthusiastically by the Missouri Company, and encouraged by the officials of Spanish Louisiana, had not been accomplished, it is of interest to note that the Spaniards paved the way for the achievement of the Americans. It is reasonable to suppose that, had Spain continued its role in the upper Mississippi Valley, the undertaking would before long have been accomplished by her subjects.[33]

14.

Three Cheers

Illinoisans cheered from the shore as boats headed across the
Mississippi to the mouth of the Missouri River late on the afternoon of May 14, 1804. Relief at getting away after almost six
months in garrison, and anxiety about the unknown journey ahead
must have represented the feelings of William Clark and about 50
men who started from Camp Dubois. Surely Corps members felt
the kind of rush like that of stepping off the high diving board, or
parachuting from an airplane at 20,000 feet.

As the party pushed away from Camp Dubois, at least six
members started journals of the voyage. In addition to Lewis and
Clark, the writers were Sergeants Ordway and Floyd, and Privates
Gass and Whitehouse. Gass became a sergeant after the death of
Floyd. Others may have kept journals or diaries, but none has
been found. All the Corps journalists, including Clark, wrote of
the departure.[1] Ordway said 38 "hands" and three sergeants, not
including Lewis and Clark, were aboard. Whitehouse wrote, "a
number of the Inhabitants from Goshen settlement came to see us
start. . . ."[2]

In spite of the thrill of being under way, work still needed to
be done. Clark and the crew wanted to see if the loads shifted, or
needed to be re-loaded for balance. At St. Charles, they added
more provisions and two additional members to the party. Through

the launch period Lewis remained in St. Louis. He had business to conclude in town before joining the crew and at the last minute also supervised departure of Osage Indian chiefs and Pierre Chouteau for a meeting with President Jefferson in Washington. When finished, Lewis planned to ride a horse to St. Charles and join the Corps of Discovery.

After Clark marked the mouth of the Dubois River as the "point of departure" for his scientific readings, the boats went only about four miles up the Missouri River for camp on the first day. It rained as they left Illinois, and it rained overnight at the first camp.[3] They experienced typical Midwest spring weather: Sunny part of the day, rainy another, and often stormy with wind and lightning. The river ran high with runoff.

The Corps made a little more than nine miles on day two, and camped at a place Clark called "Mr. Piper's Landing," named for James Piper who had lived on the river since arriving in the late 1790s.[4] May 16 dawned clear and fair, and by noon the boats pulled into St. Charles, the first white settlement on the Missouri dating from 1769.[5] People stretched along the north bank of the river to greet the voyagers. Many of the residents of St. Charles, French and Indians, cheered and welcomed the flotilla. Privates Pierre Cruzette and Francois Labiche, boatmen with needed language skills, waited with the well wishers to join the permanent party. They may have been recruited earlier, but did not spend the winter at Camp Dubois.

While the crew waited on Lewis, the next three days were a festival of fun, work and routine duty. The crew loaded provisions, rearranged loads on the boats and looked for game. Meanwhile, residents entertained the crew at the docks, furnished vegetables and held parties at which the men danced with local women. Whitehouse described the festivities: "In the Evening we were amused at a Ball, which was attended by a number of the French ladies, who were remarkably fond of dancing."[6]

Clark took time during the lulls to write his brother-in-law William Croghan, who lived in Kentucky. As the expedition got under way Croghan was the only person known to have received a written account from Clark. The captain's letter said, "My rout is uncertain. I think it more than probable that Capt. Lewis or my self will return by sea, the other by the same rout we proceed, the time is uncertain."[7] Clark could have added that uncertainty hung over the Corps like a cloud. On May 18 Clark sent Drouillard to St. Louis with a message for Lewis, telling him the boats had arrived at St. Charles and they awaited him.[8] That day, and Saturday, more visitors came to see the crew and Clark—and the weather remained lousy.

Discipline problems and restlessness plagued the crew during the brief stay. Pvt. John Collins was convicted of being absent without leave, misbehaving at a party and using disrespectful language with Clark. William Werner and Hugh Hall also were tried and found guilty of being absent. Similar outbreaks occurred periodically until the party left the Mandan Villages in 1805 and the group included only permanent members.

Finally, on May 20 Lewis completed his duties in St. Louis and left about 10:30 a.m. on horseback for St. Charles. Joining him on horses and in carriages were Captain Stoddard and two of his officers, Lt. Stephen Worrell and Lt. Clarence Mulford; Auguste Chouteau; Charles Gratiot; Dr. Antoine F. Saugrain, a French scientist and physician; and other notable townsfolk, Sylvester Labbadie, James Rankin, and David Delaunay.[9] Lewis made a journal entry upon leaving St. Louis, one of the few he wrote until reaching the Mandans. "The first 5 miles of our rout laid through a beatifull high leavel and fertile prarie which incircles the town of St. Louis."[10]

That description by Lewis applied only a short while. By midday the party encountered a severe thunderstorm that caused them to seek shelter until the downpour passed. The drenched travelers finally arrived at St. Charles about 6:30 p.m.[11] Lewis brought a letter to Clark from William Croghan saying that George Rogers Clark had recovered from an illness. For the remainder of that night and the next day, Lewis and Clark made final preparations for the launch.

Work continued during much of the day May 21, but by afternoon the Corps neared the time of departure. Citizens and St. Louis well wishers gathered on the dock to cheer the party as the boats left St. Charles. The journal-keepers recorded the moment:

Clark wrote, " . . . Set out at half passed three oClock under three Cheers from the gentlemen on the bank and proceeded on. . . ."[12] Ordway observed, "Left St. Charles at 4 oClock P.m. Showerey, the men all in high Spirits. . . ."[13] Floyd recorded, "Left St. Charles at 4 oclk. P m Showery. . . ."[14] Gass noted, "At 4 o'clock in the afternoon we left this place under a salute of three cheers from the inhabitants, which we returned with three more and a discharge of three guns."[15] Whitehouse wrote, "About 4 oClock P.M. we took our departure from Saint Charles . . . we fired our Swivel, from the Bow of our boat; and gave them three Cheers. . . ."[16]

Secretary of War Dearborn received the following letter from Captain Stoddard, dated St. Louis, June 3, 1804:

"I have the pleasure to inform you, that Captain Lewis, with his party, began to ascend the Missouri from the village of St. Charles on the 21 Ultimo. I accompanied him to that village; and he was also attended by most of the principal Gentlemen in this place and vicinity. [He] began his expedition with a Barge of 18 oars, attended by two large perogues; all of which were deeply laden, and well manned. . . ."[17]

We know the journey almost by heart. The explorers labored up the Missouri to the plains and wintered at the Mandan villages through bitter cold, snow and ice. They set out on the Missouri as soon as the spring thaw arrived. About 20 or 25 people returned to St. Louis, leaving a permanent party of approximately 30. They experienced the miraculous reunion of Sacagawea and her brother in Montana, and the near disasters in the Bitterroot Mountains.

We know of their successful trip down the Columbia River to the coast, and the soggy and depressing winter at Fort Clatsop.

Starting back in the spring of 1806, they fought the mountain snows again. The captains parted company at Travelers' Rest to test different routes through Montana. Lewis took a north route on the Missouri and the Marias rivers and barely escaped a Blackfeet war party. Clark headed down the Yellowstone River, one of the first white men to lead a group on that river. The captains met below the confluence of the two great rivers for the final leg of the journey home. In September, the party returned to St. Louis to more cheers and a hero's welcome.

Virtually lost in the telling of the return trip is an incident that occurred beyond the confluence of the Yellowstone and Missouri and again raised the name of Illinois in the journals of Lewis and Clark. About three months after Lewis and Clark left for the Pacific, two men—one from the Illinois country near Cahokia, and the other from central Missouri country—began the lonely, risky trip up the Missouri River. They purposefully started after the Corps of Discovery had taken the route, intending to spend a couple of years on the upper Missouri trapping beaver then take the furs to St. Louis for cash.

One trapper was Joseph Dickson, who moved to the Illinois country from Tennessee with his wife and two small children in 1802. A trapper, farmer and hunter, Dickson settled in the Turkey Hill area of St. Clair County on the American Bottom. Years later Dickson purchased a farm in the Shiloh district near Belleville.[18] On a hunting expedition in the fall of 1802, near the Gasconade River in Missouri, Dickson met Forrest Hancock. The two shared interests in hunting, cutting timber and trapping. Hancock had settled in the region with Daniel Boone in 1799. Dickson returned a year later to hunt with Hancock, and the two decided on a Missouri River excursion.[19]

Dickson and Hancock are believed to be the first American fur traders in the wake of Lewis and Clark, and among the very earliest white trappers on the Upper Missouri and Yellowstone rivers. It is

believed Dickson and Hancock were about the third expedition to
that region following Francois Antoine Larocque and Lewis and
Clark.[20] Hancock and Dickson trapped with mixed fortunes during the winters of 1804-05 and 1805-06, after being robbed by
Indians at least once, and failing to achieve their trapping objectives. In August of 1806, Dickson and Hancock camped near the
confluence of the Missouri and Yellowstone rivers.[21]

Lewis and Clark parted at Travelers' Rest in the Bitterroot
mountains on July 3, 1806. Five weeks later Clark and his portion
of the Corps coming from the Yellowstone route and slightly ahead
of Lewis on the Missouri, spotted a canoe on the shore and stopped.
They had discovered Dickson and Hancock, the first white men
other than the Corps Clark had seen since leaving the Mandan
villages in 1805. Everyone talked a bit, and the trappers told of
their experiences. Sgt. Ordway wrote in his journal, "about 8 A.M.
we met two trappers Americans by the names of Jos Dixon &
forest Handcock they were from the Ellynoise country . . . they
had about 20 odd good traps and tools for building canoes. . . ."[22]
Clark and crew left the two trappers and headed on down river.

A day later Lewis and his contingent arrived at the campsite of
Dickson and Hancock. Lewis wrote, "I directed the perogue and
canoes to come too at this place and found it to be the camp of two
hunters from the Illinois by name Joseph Dickson and Forest
Hancock. these men informed me that Capt. C. had passed them
about noon the day before. they also informed me that they had
left the Illinois in the summer of 1804. . . ."[23] In an effort to be
helpful, Lewis gave them a description of the Missouri River, a list
of distances to the best looking streams and "pointed out to them
the places where the beaver most abounded. . . ."

Lewis talked with the trappers about an hour and a half, and
during that time two members of the Corps, Privates Collins and
Colter, who had been absent for several days on a hunting trip,
rejoined the crew. As Lewis began his pursuit of Clark down stream,
Dickson and Hancock decided to go with them to the Mandan
villages. Colter and Hancock may have known each other from

earlier days in Ohio when Hancock assisted Boone, and Colter worked with frontiersman Simon Kenton. Enroute to the reunion of Lewis and Clark, and then to the Mandans, Hancock and Dickson regaled the Corps with stories of trapping and the fortunes that could be made.[24] They obviously got the attention of Colter. Clark provided this account of what happened next:

"Colter one of our men expressed a desire to join Some trappers who offered to become Shearers [sharers] with and furnish traps &C. the offer a very advantagious one, to him, his Services Could be dispensed with from this down and as we were disposed to be of Service to any one of our party who had performed their duty as well as Colter had done. . . ."[25]

Lewis and Clark supplied Colter and the trappers with powder and lead and other useful items, and on August 15 the trio left the Corps and headed up the Missouri. The story of Dickson, Hancock and Colter as trappers together did not have a happy ending. The three quarreled, and Colter and Hancock split from Dickson that winter. Alone near the Yellowstone, Dickson suffered a severe case of snow blindness and other deprivations. Miraculously, he survived and returned to St. Louis alone in a small boat in 1807 with enough furs to make a handsome profit and buy a farm. Colter established his own legend in the Montana and Wyoming regions and later joined with other expedition veterans in fur trading. No trace of Hancock has been discovered.[26]

The Corps of Discovery, bedraggled and mission-weary as they drew closer to the Mississippi, moved as fast as humanly possible down the Missouri River. The closer they got to St. Louis the more anxious everyone became to get home. On September 21, 1806, about 4 p.m. the boats arrived at St. Charles to a wild greeting by citizens. Many in the party fired their blunderbusses and small arms, and "we were met by great numbers of the inhabitants, we found them excessively polite."[27] They stayed overnight at St. Charles, then wasted no time shoving off in the morning. In a hard rain they stopped at Bellefontaine in north St. Louis County and received a salute of guns. They remained overnight.

In wet and disagreeable weather the party departed Bellefontaine after breakfast on September 23 and soon came to the mouth of the Missouri. The Corps made a ceremonial stop on the Wood River where they had camped more than two years earlier, then started toward St. Louis on the final short leg of the expedition. About noon they arrived in St. Louis where Clark recorded, "we Suffered the party to fire off their pieces as a Salute to the Town," and " . . . received a harty welcom from it's inhabitants. . . ."[28]

After the welcome from St. Louis citizens Lewis and Clark accepted the generosity of Pierre Chouteau and took rooms at the St. Louisan's house. Lewis immediately sent a messenger to John Hay in Cahokia to hold the outgoing mail a day so the captain could send a letter to President Jefferson. That may have been the first indication Hay and the Cahokians had of the Corps' arrival.

In the letter, dated September 23—Jefferson did not receive it until October 24—Lewis wrote: "In obedience to your orders we have penitrated the Continent of North American to the Pacific Ocean, and sufficiently explored the interior of the country to affirm with confidence that we have discovered the most practicable rout which does exist across the continent by means of the navigable branches of the Missouri and Columbia Rivers."[29]

With formalities out of the way, Lewis faced the facts. He told Jefferson the disappointing news: They found no all-water route to the Pacific and no Missouri River drainage to the Pacific. They accomplished many of their goals, however, and Lewis recited them for Jefferson. Ever thoughtful about his co-captain, Lewis wrote of Clark's contribution to the expedition:

> With rispect to the exertions and services rendered by that estseemable man Capt. William Clark in the course of late voyage I cannot say too much; if sir any credit be due for the success of that ardous enterprize in which we have been

> mutually engaged, he is equally with myself entitled to your
> consideration and that of our common country.

Having finally received and absorbed Lewis's first report,
Jefferson started a letter on October 26 to Lewis: "I recieved, my
dear Sir, with unspeakable joy, your letter of Sep. 23. . . ."[30] Jefferson
and Lewis did not have an opportunity to sit down face-to-face
and discuss the journey until December 28.

While the captains and crew unloaded the boats and questioned St. Louisans about what happened while they were absent,
the congratulations continued. On the night of September 25, a
huge celebration occurred at Christy's Tavern in St. Louis.[31] There
is no record of who attended, but they must have held off a couple
of days for people to arrive from Kaskaskia and Cahokia, and maybe
even near the Wood River. This delay would have allowed Hay,
Nicholas Jarrot, Shadrach Bond, William Morrison, John Edgar,
Pierre Menard and other Illinoisans to pay their respects to the
Corps of Discovery.

Participants made 17 toasts during the dinner and boisterous
ball that followed, with the first to Thomas Jefferson: "The friend
of science, the polar star of discovery, the philosopher and the
patriot." After the captains retired, the revelers offered the evening's
final toast to "Captains Lewis and Clark—Their perilous service
endears them to every American heart."

Curiosity remains about the fate of those that made the Pacific
journey and returned. There is specific information about only a
handful of the party, including Lewis and Clark. Many of the soldiers faded from sight almost immediately, and others left temporary footprints in the Illinois countryside. The after-lives of Lewis
and Clark have been chronicled fully as part of the saga. Each
received special treatment, promotions and assignments from President Jefferson and Congress.[32] Their lives also were intertwined
with complicated and frustrating attempts to publish the journals. A version of the captains' journals, edited by Nicholas Biddle,
was published in 1814.

The saddest story of the expedition aftermath involved the final years of Meriwether Lewis's life. Erratic behavior and poor performance as governor of Louisiana Territory were only part of the tale. He made bad personal investments and suffered financial setbacks. Through all the tribulation, Lewis is thought to have become an alcoholic, which led to a breakdown in personal relationships. His personal and public life in shambles, Lewis died on October 11, 1809, at Grinder's Inn on the Natchez Trace about 70 miles from Nashville, Tennessee.[33] The events of that stay at the Inn and the circumstances of his life and death have fueled speculation for decades about the cause of death. Consensus is that he committed suicide. The journals still had not been published, and would not be seen by the public for another five years thanks entirely to efforts of Clark.

Clark settled almost immediately in St. Louis, where he remained until his death on September 1, 1838. He married Julia Hancock and they reared a large family, naming their first child Meriwether Lewis Clark. Julia died June 27, 1820, and Clark married Harriet Radford in 1821. He served as superintendent of Indian affairs for Louisiana Territory, and had an unhappy experience in early Missouri territorial politics. Nevertheless, he remained one of the region's most popular citizens among those who remembered his feats with Lewis.

As for the rest of the Corps, little is known about most individuals. A few remained in Illinois or Missouri territories, or used that region as a base for adventures. There are two reference points for members of the party who spent time after the exploration in Illinois and Missouri. One is the pioneer history written by John Reynolds.[34] The other is a document prepared by Clark sometime between 1826 and 1829 that gives sketchy information about many in the permanent party.[35]

Reynolds listed the names of individuals who returned to Illinois after the expedition. He provided no details or timeline for their residency. Those who Reynolds said returned to the area, with additional information provided by Clark and others, were:

Private John B. Thompson; Private John Collins, returned to St. Louis and died before 1823; Private Alexander Hamilton Willard, lived in Missouri until 1852 when he moved to Sacramento, California; Private John Newman, lived around St. Louis and was killed in 1838 by Yankton Sioux Indians; Private Richard Windsor, reported living on the Sangamon River in central Illinois in the 1820s; Private Robert Frazier, died in Franklin County, Missouri, after living along the Gasconade River; and Private George Gibson, died in St. Louis in 1809.

As listed in the Clark document—with additional information from historians—these individuals spent time in Illinois or Missouri after September, 1806: Sergeant John Ordway, settled in Missouri; Private John Boley, settled near St. Louis, accompanied Zebulon Pike on two explorations; Private William Bratton, lived in Missouri; Private Francois Labiche, still alive in the St. Louis area after 1828; Private George Shannon, returned to Missouri to conclude a high profile legal career; and Private John Shields, trapped fur in Missouri with Daniel Boone and moved to Indiana.

The one member of the party about whom more details are known is George Drouillard. After returning he became among the first fur trappers to work the Upper Missouri River after Lewis and Clark, in league with people from the Illinois country who had helped the captains prepare for the expedition.

Trader Manuel Lisa, inspired by the verbal accounts of Lewis and Clark, organized an expedition for the winter of 1806-07 to the Upper Missouri in partnership with Kaskaskia businessmen Pierre Menard and William Morrison. Lisa had difficulty finding St. Louisans to finance his expedition, so he turned to the Illinoisans. He had known Menard from their earlier days in Vincennes. Menard and Morrison did not accompany Lisa on the excursion, but designated Drouillard as their agent. The surviving papers of Menard indicate that John Potts, Peter Weiser and John Robinson, all veterans of the Corps, accompanied Drouillard. En route to the Upper Missouri the expedition encountered John Colter, who had left the Corps in August, 1806, to trap on the Missouri. He joined the Lisa group. Drouillard made a second excursion with trappers to the Upper Missouri in 1810. Blackfeet Indians harassed the group in May and ambushed and killed Drouillard.[36]

Drouillard emerged from the Lewis and Clark expedition as one of a few who received special mention and accolades from the captains. Historians have acclaimed him as one of two or three most valuable members of the party. Lewis said of Drouillard:

> A man of much merit; he has been peculiarly usefull from his knowledge of the common language of gesticulation, and his uncommon skill as a hunter and woodsman; those several duties he performed in good faith, and with an ardor which deserves the highest commendation. It was his fate also to have encountered, on various occasions, with either Captain Clark or myself, all the most dangerous and trying scenes of the voyage, in which he uniformly acquitted himself with honor. . . . [37]

But for their moment of glory as members of the Corps of Discovery, the men of Lewis and Clark were representative of the thousands of Americans who roamed and explored the frontier just before and after the Louisiana Purchase. This also can be said of Meriwether Lewis and William Clark. They would have been little known or remembered were it not for the extraordinary journey to the Pacific. This is not to diminish their feat, but rather to acknowledge their place at the head of the great migration of Americans west of the Mississippi. The Corps of Discovery's achievement ranks at the top of the list of American explorations for succeeding against overwhelming odds and for leaving records of the journey for future generations to ponder. For their part in the historic exploration, people of the Illinois country can justifiably claim a full measure of pride.

NOTES

1. A Vast Enterprise

1. The crew began building Fort Mandan on 3 November 1804, and left on the journey to the Pacific on 7 April 1805. Gary Moulton, editor, *The Journals of the Lewis and Clark Expedition* (Lincoln: University of Nebraska Press, 1987), 3:2-4. Hereafter Moulton's work, now the accepted standard of scholarship, will be cited as JLCE. The crew began work on Fort Clatsop near the Pacific coast on 7 December 1805, and departed on the return trip 23 March 1806. JLCE, 6:2.

2. Donald Jackson, editor, *Letters of the Lewis and Clark Expedition with Related Documents, 1783-1854,* two volumes, second edition (Urbana: University of Illinois Press, 1978), 2:655-56.

3. Donald Jackson, *Thomas Jefferson & the Stony Mountain: Exploring the West from Monticello* (Urbana: University of Illinois Press, 1981), 119.

4. Jefferson's Message to Congress, 18 January 1803, Jackson, ed., *Letters,* 1:10-13.

5. Harry Ammon, *James Monroe: The Quest for National Identity* (New York: McGraw-Hill, 1971), 203-224; Jackson, *Stony Mountains,* 98-99.

6. Jefferson's Instructions to Lewis, 20 June 1803, Jackson, ed., *Letters,* 1:61-66; Paul Russell Cutright, *Lewis and Clark: Pioneering Naturalists* (Urbana: University of Illinois, 1969), 1-9.

7. Jackson, *Stony Mountains,* 139.

8. Clark to Lewis, 18 July 1803, Jackson, ed., *Letters,* 1:111.

9. Lewis to Clark, 19 July 1803, Jackson, ed., *Letters,* 1:57-60.

10. Clark to Lewis, 18 July 1803, Jackson, ed., *Letters,* 1:110.

11. John Logan Allen, *Passage Through the Garden: Lewis and Clark and the Image of the American Northwest* (Urbana: University of Illinois Press, 1975), 170.

12. Allen, *Passage,* 171.

13. Allen, *Passage,* 180.

14. James P. Ronda, *Lewis and Clark Among the Indians* (Lincoln: University of Nebraska Press, 1984), 10.

15. Ronda, *Indians,* 10-11, 14.

16. Clark to Jefferson, 24 July 1803, Jackson, ed., *Letters,* 1:113.

2. The Illinois Country

1. Clarence Walworth Alvord, *Illinois Country, 1673-1818* (Urbana: University of Illinois Press, 1987, reprint) 407; James E. Davis, *Frontier Illinois* (Bloomington: Indiana University Press, 1998) 115-16.

2. Ibid.

3. John Reynolds, *Pioneer History* (Belleville: N.A. Randall, 1852), 249-50.

4. John Francis McDermott, ed., "The Western Journals of George Hunter," *Transactions of the American Philosophical Society,* 53, July, 1963, 28-29.

5. Alvord, *Illinois Country,* 8.

6. John W. Allen, *Legends and Lore of Southern Illinois* (Carbondale: Southern Illinois University Press, 1963), 303-04.

7. Charles J. Bareis and James W. Porter, *American Bottom Archaeology* (Urbana: University of Illinois Press, 1993), 16-17.

8. Alvord, *Illinois Country,* 133.

9. Bareis and Porter, *American Bottom,* 32.

10. McDermott, ed., "George Hunter," 30.

11. George P. Garrison, editor, "A Memorandum of M. Austin's Journey," *American Historical Review,* 1900, 5:539.

12. Davis, *Frontier Illinois*, 82, 83; Robert P. Howard, *Illinois: A History of the Prairie State* (Grand Rapids: Eerdmans Publishing Company, 1972), 57, 58; Alvord, *Illinois Country*, 359, 369-370.

13. Howard, *Illinois*, 57-58.

14. John Francis McDermott, "Cahokia and Its People," *Old Cahokia: A Narrative and Documents Illustrating the First Century of Its History* (St. Louis: Historical Documents Foundation, 1949), 1-11; Charles E. Peterson, "Notes on Old Cahokia," *Journal of the Illinois State Historical Society*, March, 1948, 8-12.

15. Davis, *Frontier Illinois*, 53-54; Peterson, "Notes on Old Cahokia," 14; Alvord, *Illinois Country*, 202.

16. Alvord, *Illinois Country*, 131-32; Davis, *Frontier Illinois*, 41.

17. Howard, *Illinois*, 118-20.

18. Alvord, *Illinois Country*; Howard, *Illinois*, 39-43; Rose Jo Boylan, *East St. Louis Journal*, 20 February 1964, and 24 June 1964, archives, Southern Illinois University-Edwardsville; Davis, *Frontier Illinois*; Walter J. Saucier and Kathrine Wagner Seineke, "Francois Saucier, Engineer of Fort de Chartres, Illinois," *Frenchmen and French Ways in the Mississippi Valley*, 224-227.

19. John Francis McDermott, "Auguste Chouteau: First Citizen of Upper Louisiana," *Frenchmen and French Ways in the Mississippi Valley* (Urbana: University of Illinois Press, 1969), 1-13.

20. John Francis McDermott, "The Frontier Re-Examined," *The Frontier Re-Examined* (Urbana: University of Illinois Press, 1967), 3-6.

3. The First Clark

1. Stephen E. Ambrose, *Undaunted Courage: Meriwether Lewis, Thomas Jefferson and the Opening of the American West* (New York: Simon and Schuster, 1996). According to existing correspondence, Clark had spent time in Washington, D.C., during 1800, 1801 and 1802, where he met with Lewis and became acquainted with Jefferson, John Louis Loos, "A Biography of William Clark, 1770-1813," doctoral dissertation, Washington University, St. Louis, 63.

2. A pirogue is a canoe made by hollowing out a log. In their journals Lewis and Clark discuss a "white" pirogue and a "red" pirogue, the former being the smaller of the two, JLCE, *Journals,* 2:215n.

3. Alvord, *Illinois Country,* 323.

4. Rose Jo Boylan, "Clark Occupied Cahokia, Kaskaskia at Age 25," *East St. Louis Journal,* 29 December 1967, 8.

5. Reynolds, *Pioneer History of Illinois,* 71-72.

6. Theodore Calvin Pease and Marguerite Jenison Pease, *George Rogers Clark and the Revolution in Illinois, 1763-1787* (Springfield: Illinois State Historical Library, 1929), 43n.

7. There are many accounts of Clark's triumphs in Kaskaskia, Cahokia and Vincennes. Some of value are: Kathrine Wagner Seineke, *The George Rogers Clark Adventure in the Illinois* (New Orleans: Polyanthos, 1981); Alvord, *Illinois Country;* Reynolds, *Pioneer History;* Milo M. Quaife, editor, *The Conquest of Illinois* (Chicago, 1920); John D. Barnhart, *Henry Hamilton and George Rogers Clark in the American Revolution, with Unpublished Journal of Lieut. Gov. Henry Hamilton* (Crawfordsville, 1951); Pease, *Clark;* James Alton James, "George Rogers Clark Papers, 1771-1781," *Collections of the Illinois State Historical Library* (Springfield, 1912) volume 8.

8. Interview by Lyman C. Draper of Pashal Leon Cerre, October 1846, Draper Collections of Clark mss, volume 8, Wisconsin State Historical Society Library, Madison; St. Louis, Missouri, Gabriel Cerre Papers, Missouri Historical Society, Missouri History Museum, Library and Research Center, St. Louis.

9. Pease, *Clark*, 45-47.

10. Howard, *Illinois*, 50; Pease, *Clark*, 46.

11. Theophile Papin, Jr., biographical sketch of Charles Gratiot, Gratiot Papers, Missouri Historical Society, St. Louis, no date.

12. Pease, *Clark*, 49-50.

13. John Bakeless, *Background to Glory* (Philadelphia: Lippincott, 1957), 85-86; Edna Kenton, *Simon Kenton: His Life and Period, 1755-1836* (New York: Doubleday, 1930), 97; Allan W. Eckert, *The Frontiersmen: A Narrative* (Boston: Little, Brown, 1967), 143-44.

14. Before leaving for Vincennes Clark bought a Mississippi River flatboat, armed it and christened it the *Willing*. He sent 40 of his 175 soldiers on the boat. Delayed by weather, the flatboat reached Vincennes via the Ohio and Wabash rivers after the conquest of Fort Sackville, Davis, *Frontier Illinois*, 73.

15. Seineke, *George Rogers Clark Adventure*, "Clark's Account of the Capture of Vincennes and the Articles of Capitulation of Fort Sackville," 350-354; Hamilton to Lord Shelburne, 9 April 1782, Shelburne Manuscripts, volume 66, transcription of original for C. M. Burton, 1922, Burton Historical Collections, Detroit Public Library, 1-20; also James, "George Rogers Clark Papers, 1771-1781"; and Pease, *George Rogers Clark*, 51-54.

16. Palmer, *Clark of the Ohio*, 386-387.

17. Seineke, "Clark's Account of the Capture of Vincennes," *George Rogers Clark Adventure*, 353.

18. Hamilton to Shelburne, 9 April 1782, 12-13, Burton Historical Collections.

19. Jefferson to George Rogers Clark, 4 December 1783, Jackson, ed., *Letters*, 2: 654-65.

20. George Rogers Clark to Jefferson, 8 February 1784, Jackson, ed., *Letters*, 2:655-56.

21. George Rogers Clark to Jefferson, 12 December 1802, Jackson, ed., *Letters*, 1:7-8.

4. Lewis and Clark: Frontiersmen

1. A full account of Meriwether Lewis's military history and early life is in Ambrose, *Undaunted Courage;* also, Richard Dillon, *Meriwether Lewis: A Biography* (New York: Coward, McCann, 1965).
2. Wiley Sword, *President Washington's Indian War: The Struggle for the Old Northwest, 1790-1795* (Norman: University of Oklahoma Press, 1985), 205; Ambrose, *Undaunted Courage*, 46.
3. Ambrose, *Undaunted Courage*, 44-45.
4. John Louis Loos, "William Clark's Part in the Preparation of the Lewis and Clark Expedition," *Bulletin of the Missouri Historical Society,* 1954, 490-92; Ambrose, *Undaunted Courage*, 46.
5. Loos, "Lewis and Clark Expedition," 491.
6. Jefferson to Lewis, 23 February 1801, and Lewis to Jefferson, 10 March 1801, Jackson, ed., *Letters*, 1:2, 3.
7. Information about William Clark's early years is from Loos, "Biography of William Clark," 1-9; Reuben Gold Thwaites, "William Clark, Soldier, Explorer, Statesman," *Missouri Historical Society Collections,* 1906, 2:6; Jerome O. Steffen, *William Clark: Jeffersonian Man on the Frontier* (Norman: University of Oklahoma Press, 1977), 11-19.
8. Loos, "Biography of William Clark," 11.
9. Reginald E. McGrane, editor, "William Clark's Journal of General Wayne's Campaigns," *Mississippi Valley Historical Review,* 1:418-19; Loos, "Biography of William Clark," 11.
10. Loos, "Biography of William Clark," 33-34, 36; Steffen, *Clark,* 22-24.
11. Samuel W. Thomas, "William Clark's 1795 and 1797 Journals and Their Significance," *Bulletin of the Missouri Historical Society,* 1969, 25:280; Loos, "Biography of William Clark," 50.
12. Thomas, "Clark's Journals," 279n.
13. Clark's report to General Anthony Wayne, 1-4, November 1795, Thomas "Clark's Journal," 280n.

14. Loos, "Biography of William Clark," 53; Thomas, "Clark's Journals," 281n, Clark's report.

15. Thomas, "Clark's Journals," 282n, Clark's report.

16. "The fort stood a few miles below present Wickliffe, Ballard County, Kentucky, just above Mayfield Creek, the dividing line between Ballard and Carlisle counties," JLCE, 2:94n.

17. Thomas, "Clark's Journals," 286.

18. Loos, "Biography of William Clark," 58.

19. Thomas, "Clark's Journals," 287.

20. W. A. Burt, "John Rice Jones: A Brief Sketch of the Life and Public Career of the First Practicing Lawyer of Illinois," *Chicago Historical Society's Collections,* 4:230-40; Francis S. Philbrick, *Collections of the Illinois State Historical Library: The Laws of Indiana Territory, 1801-1809* (Springfield, 1930), ccxxxviii; Reynolds, *Pioneer History,* 138-41.

21. George Rogers Clark to William Clark, 1 September 1797, Thomas, "Clark's Journals," 288n.

22. Thomas, "Clark's Journals," 289n.

23. Thomas, "Clark's Journals," 3 September 1797, 289.

24. Thomas, "Clark's Journals," 4 September 1797, 289.

25. McDermott, "George Hunter," 29-30.

26. Philbrick, *Laws of Indiana Territory,* cclxvi; Thomas, "Clark's Journals," 291.

27. Thomas, "Clark's Journals," 10 September 1797, 293.

28. Thomas, "Clark's Journals," 23 September 1797, 293.

29. Thomas, "Clark's Journals," 295.

5. The River Journey

1. Lewis to Clark, 19 June 1803, Jackson, ed., *Letters,* 1:58.

2. Charles G. Clarke, *The Men of the Lewis and Clark Expedition, a biographical roster of the fifty-one members* (Glendale: Arthur H. Clark, 1970), and Gary Moulton, JLCE, volume two, appendix A.

3. Jefferson's Instructions to Lewis, 20 June 1803, Jackson, ed., *Letters,* 1:61.

4. Financial Records of the Expedition, 5 August 1807, Jackson, ed., *Letters*, 2:419.

5. Lewis to Jefferson, 3 October 1803, Jackson, ed., *Letters*, 1:131.

6. Jefferson to Lewis, 16 November 1803, Jackson, ed., *Letters*, 1:136.

7. JLCE, 11 November 1803, 2:85.

8. M. O. Skarsten, *George Drouillard: Hunter and Interpreter for Lewis and Clark and Fur Trader, 1807-1810* (Glendale: Arthur H. Clark, 1964).

9. Ambrose, *Undaunted Courage*, 118.

10. John B. Fortier, "New Light on Fort Massac," *Frenchmen and FrenchWays in the Mississippi Valley,* John Francis McDermott, editor (Urbana: University of Illinois Press, 1969), 62.

11. Norman W. Caldwell, "Fort Massac During the French and Indian War," *Journal of the Illinois State Historical Society,* Springfield, 1951, 106; Fortier, "New Light," 61.

12. Caldwell, "Fort Massac," 118-19.

13. Fortier, "New Light," 70.

14. Henry Dearborn to Russell Bissell, Amos Stoddard, and Daniel Bissell, 2 July 1803, Jackson, ed., *Letters*, 1:103.

15. Ambrose, *Undaunted Courage*, 119; JLCE, Appendix A.

16. Ambrose, *Undaunted Courage*, 119.

17. JLCE, 2:89.

18. JLCE, 2:101.

19. Arlen Large, "Additions to the Party: How an Expedition Grew and Grew," *We Proceeded On,* 1990, 4-7.

20. JLCE, 2:105, 109n.

21. JLCE, 2:111-112.

6. Adding to the Corps

1. Henry Dearborn to Russell Bissell and Amos Stoddard, 2 July 1803, Jackson, ed., *Letters*, 1:103n.

2. Jackson, ed., *Letters,* l:103n.

3. Ernest Staples Osgood, editor, *The Field Notes of Captain William Clark, 1803-1805* (New Haven: Yale University Press, 1964), xxiv.
4. JLCE, 1:145n.
5. Lewis to Jefferson, 19 December 1803, Jackson, ed., *Letters*, 1:145.
6. Large, "Additions to the Party," 7.
7. JLCE, 2: appendix A.

7. The Kaskaskians

1. Philbrick, *Laws of Indiana Territory*, lxxxiii-lxxxv.
2. Edgar's accounts of his activities during the American Revolution are in two documents, both in the Burton Historical Collections of the Detroit Public Library, and undated. About 1813, when Edgar was approximately 80 years old, he wrote a lengthy account of his war experiences. Six or seven years later, in a pleading to Congress, he wrote a much briefer document, which summarized his years as an agent for the United States. William Stags swore to a similar account of Edgar's adventures in an affidavit dated 27 February 1828, based on conversations with Edgar in Montreal in 1781, also from the Burton Collections.
3. Biographical material about Edgar appears in footnote 48 of the appendix to Francis S. Philbrick's work on the laws of Indiana Territory. Also of value is James H. Roberts' "The Life and Times of General John Edgar," *Illinois State Historical Society Transactions*, 1907. Both rely on information from the Lyman Draper Manuscripts in the State Historical Society of Wisconsin.
4. Among the Simon Kenton Papers in the Draper Manuscripts are letters Draper received during his years of gathering information from friends and distant relatives of Mrs. Edgar.
5. Allan W. Eckert, *Frontiersmen* (Boston: Little Brown, 1967), 198.
6. George O. Tiffany to Lyman Draper, 4 December 1889, Draper MSS, 7BB, Simon Kenton Papers; Eckert, *Frontiersmen*, 198.
7. Roberts, "General John Edgar," 69.
8. Edna Kenton, *Simon Kenton*, 138.
9. Eckert, *Frontiersmen*, 194; Kenton, *Simon Kenton*, 136.

10. Eckert, *Frontiersmen*, 199; Kenton, *Simon Kenton*, 138.

11. Eckert, *Frontiersmen*, 201; Kenton, *Simon Kenton*, 139.

12. Kenton, *Simon Kenton*, 140-143; Eckert, *Frontiersmen*, 202.

13. Kenton, *Simon Kenton*, 140; Roberts, "General John Edgar," 68.

14. Stags, affidavit, 1828, 1; Edgar to Congress, 1.

15. Roberts, "General John Edgar," 67.

16. Edgar to Congress, 2; Edgar, 1813, 1,2.

17. Edgar, 1813, 7; Roberts, "General John Edgar," 67. Francis S. Philbrick says American authorities already knew of the Vermont conspiracy, *Laws of Indiana Territory*, cclxiii.

18. Edgar, 1813, 7, 8.

19. Edgar, 1813, 10.

20. Edgar to Congress, 3.

21. Edgar to Congress, 4.

22. Edgar to Congress, 3.

23. Edgar to Congress, 2.

24. Philbrick, *Laws of Indiana Territory*, cclxiv.

25. Philbrick, *Laws of Indiana Territory*, cclxiv; Roberts, "General John Edgar," 69. "He rendered many important services. His losses were very great and his sufferings still greater," *American State Papers*, Legislative and Executive, No. 56, "Refugees from Canada and Nova Scotia," 6th Congress, 1st Session, House of Representatives, 8 May 1800; No. 58, 9 May 1800.

26. Reynolds, *Pioneer History*, 91-93.

27. Philbrick, *Laws of Indiana Territory*, lxxvii.

28. John Rice Jones to Major John Francis Hamtramck, 29 October 1789, Gayle Thornbrough, editor, *Outpost on the Wabash, 1787-1791* (Indianapolis: Indiana Historical Society, 1957), 200-204.

29. Edgar to Hamtramck, 28 October 1789, Thornbrough, ed., *Outpost*, 197-200.

30. Father Jacobin Le Dru, Edgar and Citizens of Kaskaskia, to Hamtramck, 14 September 1789, Thornbrough, ed., *Outpost*, 190-191.

31. Proposition of Edgar, 3 October 1789, Thornbrough, ed., *Outpost*, 192.

32. Hamtramck to Father Le Dru and Edgar, 14 October 1789, Thornbrough, ed., *Outpost*, 193.

33. Edgar to Major Hamtramck, 28 October 1789, Thornbrough, ed., *Outpost,* 199.

34. May Allinson, "The Government of Illinois, 1790-1799," *Transactions of the Illinois State Historical Society,* 1907, 277-280; Davis, *Frontier Illinois,* 101; Howard, *Illinois,* 64-65.

35. Biographical material is from John L. Tevebaugh, "Merchant on the Western Frontier: William Morrison of Kaskaskia, 1790-1837," doctoral dissertation, University of Illinois, 1962; Philbrick, *Laws of Indiana Territory,* cclxvi; Allen, *Legends and Lore;* Reynolds, *Pioneer History;* Morrison Family Papers, Missouri Historical Society, St. Louis; and Richard Edward Ogelsby, "William Morrison," *The Mountain Men and the Fur Trade of the Far West,* (Glendale: Arthur Clark, 1966).

36. Tevebaugh, "Merchant on the Western Frontier," 22.

37. Reynolds, *Pioneer History,* 129-133.

38. Tevebaugh, "Merchant on the Western Frontier," 91.

39. Ogelsby, "William Morrison," 200.

40. Richard Edward Ogelsby, *Manuel Lisa and the Opening of the Missouri Fur Trade* (Norman: University of Oklahoma Press, 1963), 40-41; Kathrine Wagner Seineke, editor, *Pierre Menard Collection* (Springfield: Illinois State Historical Society, 1972), 15.

41. Philbrick, *Laws of Indiana Territory,* cclxvi; Alvord, *Illinois Country,* 422-427.

42. JLCE, 2:117.

8. Getting Down to Business

1. JLCE, 2:123.

2. JLCE, 2:124, 2-125n.

3. Carl R. Baldwin, *Echoes of Their Voices: A Saga of the Pioneers Who Pushed the Frontier to the Mississippi* (St. Louis: Hawthorne Publishing Co., 1978); Reynolds, *Pioneer History,* 151-156; Rose Jo Boylan, *East St. Louis Journal,* 9 January 1964, archives, Southern Illinois University-Edwardsville; J. L. McDonough, *History of Randolph, Monroe and Perry Counties, Illinois* (Philadelphia, 1883),

78-81. Current genealogical work on the Whiteside family was prepared by William R. Whiteside of Cottage Hills, Illinois, no relation to the family.

4. Reynolds, *Pioneer History*, 152.

5. Reynolds, *Pioneer History*, 188.

6. Baldwin, *Echoes*, 275-76; Reynolds, *Pioneer History*, 155; Whiteside, genealogy, 4.

7. Whiteside, William Bolin Whiteside genealogy, 2; Baldwin, *Echoes*, 277-278.

8. Boylan, *East St. Louis Journal*, "Whiteside County Was Named After Whole Colorful Clan," 9.

9. JLCE, 2:126.

10. JLCE, 2:127.

11. Lewis to Jefferson, 19 December 1803, Jackson, ed., *Letters*, 1:145.

12. Lewis to Jefferson, 19 December 1803, Jackson, ed., *Letters*, 1:145.

13. John Francis McDermott, "Myths and Realities," 1-16; "Auguste Chouteau: First Citizen of Upper Louisiana," 1-13.

14. *Annals of St. Louis: Territorial Days*, "St. Louis in 1804: The Village and Town—its Progress," 22-25, Missouri Historical Society, St. Louis.

15. John Francis McDermott, "Stoddard Discovers St. Louis," *Bulletin of the Missouri Historical Society* (1954), 10:331.

16. McDermott, "Stoddard," 333.

17. McDermott, "Stoddard," 333-334.

18. Lewis to Jefferson, 19 December 1803, Jackson, ed., *Letters*, 144.

19. Carlos Dehault Delassus to Juan Manuel de Salcedo and the Marques de Casa Calvo, 9 December 1803, Jackson, ed., *Letters*, 143.

20. Delassus to Salcedo and Calvo, 9 December 1803, Jackson, ed., *Letters*, 1:142.

21. Lewis to Jefferson, 19 December 1803, Jackson, ed., *Letters*, 1:147.

22. Everett L. Sparks, "Where the Trail Begins: The Illinois Legacy to the Lewis and Clark Expedition," *We Proceeded On*, February 1988, 8; Ambrose, *Undaunted Courage*, 123.

23. Financial Records of the Expedition, 5 August 1807, Jackson, ed., *Letters*, 2:423.

24. JLCE, 2:129.

25. Jefferson to Lewis, 16 November 1803, Jackson, ed., *Letters*, 1:137.

9. The Cahokians

1. Reynolds, *Pioneer History,* 50.

2. Reynolds, *Pioneer History,* 51.

3. Papin, Jr., biographical sketch, "Charles Gratiot," Gratiot Papers; Cahokia Records, Charles Gratiot, P4-N2; Reynolds, *Pioneer History,* 254-259; Osgood, *Field Notes,* 9n.

4. Charles Gratiot to David Gratiot, 8 October 1774, Brenda R. Geiseker, "A Business Venture at Cahokia: The Letters of Charles Gratiot, 1778-1779," *Old Cahokia: A Narrative and Documents Illustrating the First Century of Its History,* 190.

5. Charles Gratiot to David Gratiot, 8 October 1774, Geiseker, "A Business Venture," 190.

6. Geiseker, "A Business Venture," 192.

7. McDermott, "Cahokia and Its People," *Old Cahokia.* 30.

8. Charles E. Peterson, "Notes on Old Cahokia," *Journal of the Illinois State Historical Society,* 42:316.

9. William E. Foley and C. David Rice, *The First Chouteaus: River Barons of Early St. Louis* (Urbana: University of Illinois Press, 1983), 38.

10. Papin, "Charles Gratiot," 3.

11. Meriwether Lewis to Amos Stoddard, 16 May 1804, Jackson, ed., *Letters,* 191.

12. Reynolds, *Pioneer History,* 258.

13. Papin, "Charles Gratiot," 2.

14. Margaret E. Babb, "The Mansion House of Cahokia and Its Builder—Nicholas Jarrot," *Transactions of the Illinois State Historical Society,* 1924, 78-93; Baldwin, *Echoes,* 58-75; Reynolds, *Pioneer History,* 175-179; Adolph B. Suess, *The Romantic Story of Cahokia, Illinois* (Belleville: Buechler Publishing Co., 1949), 19-22, 72-79; Philbrick, *Laws of Indiana Territory,* cclix-cclx.

15. Reynolds, *Pioneer History,* 175.

16. Howard, *Illinois,* 84.

17. Helen Clanton, "Restoring 150-Year-Old Cahokia Home," *St. Louis Post Dispatch*, 18 April 1945, Tiffany Papers, Missouri Historical Society, St. Louis; Babb, "Mansion House," 80-83.

18. Baldwin, *Echoes*, 58-59.

19. Babb, "Mansion House," 83.

20. Alvord, *Illinois Country*, 434, 438.

21. Reynolds, *Pioneer History*, 176.

22. Reynolds, *Pioneer History*, 177.

23. The record of land claims filed by Jarrot, appearing in Brink, *History of Madison County, Illinois* (Edwardsville, 1882,) 68-70, reveals the extent to which he owned or claimed to own land in the region before it became Madison County.

24. Philbrick, *Laws of Indiana Territory*, lxxxiii-lxxxvi.

25. Bareis and Porter, *American Bottom*, 187-189.

26. Babb, "Mansion House," 89; Baldwin, *Echoes*, 64; Clanton, *Post-Dispatch*.

27. Horatio Ball to Madam Jarrot, "List of land entered on the auditors books in the name of N. Jarrot," 15 July 1926, Missouri Historical Society, Tiffany Family Papers, St. Louis.

10. The Indispensable Man

1. Jackson, ed., *Letters*, 1:156n-57n; Osgood, ed., *Field Notes*, 16n.

2. Sources include Reynolds, *Pioneer History*, Jackson, ed., *Letters*, Philbrick, *Laws of Indiana Territory*, and the local history writings of Rose Jo Boylan.

3. In journals and notes by Lewis and Clark from 13 December 1803, to 14 May 1804, John Hay is mentioned 13 separate times, JLCE. Hay is mentioned in two other documents written by Lewis and Clark during that time period, Jackson, ed., *Letters*.

4. Reynolds, *Pioneer History*, 191.

5. Information from the Burton Collections, Detroit Public Library, documents Jehu Hay's lengthy military career and administrative experiences.

6. Davis, *Frontier Illinois*, 68.

7. Milo M. Quaife, "Detroit Biographies: Jehu Hay," *Burton Historical Collection Leaflet*, (1929), 8:1-16.

8. Reynolds, *Pioneer History*, 188.

9. Quaife, "Jehu Hay," 2-5.

10. William L. Jenks, "Diary of the Siege of Detroit," *Michigan History Magazine*, (1928), 12:437-442.

11. Quaife, "Jehu Hay," 7.

12. Quaife, "A Narrative of Life on the Old Frontier: Henry Hay's Journal from Detroit to the Mississippi River," *Indiana Historical Society Publications*, 1921, 214n, 243n; Quaife, "Jehu Hay," 7-8.

13. Hamilton to Lord Shelburne, 9 April 1782, 18, Burton Historical Collections.

14. Quaife, "Jehu Hay," 11.

15. Clarence M. Burton, editor, *The City of Detroit Michigan, 1701-1922* (Detroit: Clarke Publishing Co., 1922), Burton Historical Collections, 1:132.

16. Burton, *City of Detroit*, 1:133; Quaife, "Jehu Hay," 12; Haldimand to Lt. Col. De Peyster, 30 October 1783, Burton, *City of Detroit*, 1:396.

17. Hay to Hamilton, 25 October 1784, Burton Collections, Otto Fisher Papers, 2; Hay to Hamilton, 20 November 1784, Burton Collections, Fisher Papers; Hay to Hamilton, 24 March 1785, Burton Collections, Hay Papers.

18. Reynolds, *Pioneer History*, 188.

19. Reynolds, *Pioneer History*, 189.

20. Abraham Nasatir, *Borderland in Retreat: From Spanish Louisiana to the Far Southwest*, (Albuquerque: University of New Mexico Press, 1976), 11-67; Marjorie Wilkins Campbell, *The North West Company* (New York: St. Martin's Press, 1957), 1-2; W. L. Morton, *Manitoba: A History* (Toronto: University of Toronto Press, 1967), 39-40; Morton, "The North West Company: Pedlars Extraordinary," *Aspects of the Fur Trade, 1967*, Minnesota Historical Society, 10-15; Hiram Chittenden, *A History of the American Fur Trade of the Far West* (Stanford: Academic Reprints, 1954) 1:88.

21. Report of Francois Luis Hector Carondelet, 8 January 1796, Nasatir, ed., *Before Lewis and Clark,* 2:407.

22. Nasatir, "The Anglo-Spanish Frontier on the Upper Mississippi, 1786-1796," *The Iowa Journal of History and Politics,* 1931, 55-200; Carondelet: Instructions to Zenon Trudeau, 28 March 1792, Nasatir, ed., *Before Lewis and Clark,* 1:151-153.

23. Reynolds, *Pioneer History,* 190.

24. Reynolds, *Pioneer History,* 190.

25. M. M. Quaife, "Extracts from Capt. McKay's Journal—and Others," *Wisconsin Historical Society Proceedings,* 1916, 202-209. The documents edited by Quaife include extracts from Mackay's journal, notes on the extracts by Hay and Hay's journal of the trip from Mackinac to the Souris River country. McDermott's handwritten notes in Box 28, File 21, McDermott Collection, Southern Illinois University-Edwardsville, Lovejoy Library, read, "The person who made the extracts had the use of the original Mackay document is clear from the endorsement. . .The extractor was quite possibly John Hay of Cahokia for attached to it were notes by Hay and also a journal of a trip by Hay. . .along the shores of Lake Superior in 1794. Of course, some person other than Hay, having access to both Mackay and Hay material could have completed the notes. . ."

26. Quaife, "Extract from Capt. McKay's Journal," 205.

27. Quaife, "Extract from Capt. McKay's Journal," 207.

28. Carondelet to Alcudia, 8 January 1796, 387, Nasatir, ed., *Before Lewis and Clark,* and 1:403n-404n.

29. Nasatir, "Jacques Clamorgan," *The Mountain Men and the Fur Trade in the Far West,* (Glendale: Arthur H. Clark, 1966), 82.

30. Nasatir, "Clamorgan," 83.

31. Nasatir, ed., *Before Lewis and Clark,* 2:464-469.

32. Nasatir, "Clamorgan," 85.

33. Nasatir, ed., *Before Lewis and Clark,* 1: 87-93.

34. Juan Ventura Morales to Diego Maria Gardoqui, New Orleans, 1 December 1796, Nasatir, ed., *Before Lewis and Clark,* 2: 481-482.

35. Memorial of Clamorgan to Trudeau, St. Louis, 27 September 1798, Nasatir, ed., *Before Lewis and Clark,* 571-572.

36. Quaife, "Jehu Hay," 15.
37. Philbrick, *Laws of Indiana Territory,* cclxii-cclxiii.
38. Reynolds, *Pioneer History,* 190.
39. Philbrick, *Laws of Indiana Territory,* cclxiii; Rose Jo Boylan, "John Hay: Mr. St. Clair County," *East St. Louis Journal,* 16 May 1963, 9.
40. Philbrick, *Laws of Indiana Territory,* ccxlv; Reynolds, *Pioneer History,* 191.
41. John Reynolds, "Brief History of Belleville," from Revised Ordinances of the City of Belleville, 1862, *Journal of the St. Clair County Historical Society,* 1966, 39.
42. Solon J. Buck, *Illinois in 1818* (Urbana: University of Illinois Press, 1967), 191; J. P. Dunn, Jr., *Indiana: A Redemption from Slavery,* (Boston: Houghton Mifflin, 1888), 365; Philbrick, *Laws of Indiana Territory,* ccxlv.
43. Reynolds, *Pioneer History,* 192.
44. Rose Jo Boylan, "When St. Clair Stood Alone," *Journal of the St. Clair Historical Society,* 1965, 11.
45. Philbrick, *Laws of Indiana Territory,* ccxlv.
46. Boylan, "John Hay: Mr. St. Clair County," 9.
47. *Belleville Weekly Advocate,* 20 October 1842.
48. Reynolds, "Brief History of Belleville," 39.
49. Baldwin, *Echoes,* 119.

11. On to Camp Dubois

1. JLCE, 2:131.
2. Paul Russell Cutright, *A History of the Lewis and Clark Journals* (Norman: University of Oklahoma Press, 1976), 145-76.
3. Osgood, ed., *Field Notes,* xiii-xxxv; JLCE 1:133n.
4. Brink, *History of Madison County,* 71-80.
5. Rose Jo Boylan, "Land of Goshen Settled," *East St. Louis Journal,* 15 July 1962; Baldwin, *Echoes,* 339; Whiteside, William B. Whiteside genealogy, 4, states first landowners in Madison County included

William B. Whiteside "on the bluffs in what appears to have been the most attractive part of the county, the 'Goshen' settlement."

6. Osgood, ed., *Notes,* 11, 14, 27.

7. William R. Whiteside to author, 28 January, 2000.

8. Brink, *History of Madison County,* 71-72, 77.

9. Lewis to Clark, 17 December 1803, Jackson, ed., *Letters,* 1:144.

10. Osgood, ed., *Notes,* 8.

11. Osgood, ed., *Notes,* 11.

12. Jackson, ed., *Letters,* 1:145n.

13. Brink, *History of Madison County,* 72.

14. Everett L. Sparks, "Where the Trail Begins: The Illinois Legacy to the Lewis and Clark Expedition," *We Proceeded On,* September, 1988, 4-9; Rev. Thomas E. Lippincott, "Early Days in Madison County," Manuscript Papers (No. 4) Southern Illinois University-Edwardsville, Lovejoy Library.

15. Sparks, "Trail," 7.

16. Roy E. Appleman, *Lewis and Clark's Transcontinental Exploration, 1804-1806,* (Washington, D.C.: National Park Service, 2000) revised, 287.

17. Robert C. Fietsam, Jr., "The Lewis and Clark Expedition Winter Base of Operations at Camp DuBois," *Journal of the St. Clair County Historical Society,* 1966, 16-17.

18. Sparks, "Trail," 6.

19. Sparks, "Trail," 6.

20. John Francis McDermott, "William Clark's Struggle with Place Names in Upper Louisiana," *The Bulletin of the Missouri Historical Society,* 1978, 34:143-146.

21. Osgood, ed., *Notes,* 11.

22. Clark to William Crogham, 15 January 1804, Jackson, ed., *Letters,* 1:164.

23. Osgood, ed., *Notes,* 15.

24. JLCE, 9:366.

25. Lippincott, "Early Days," 4.

26. Lippincott, "Early Days," 1.

27. Lippincott, "Early Days," 2.

28. Lippincott, "Early Days," Letter 4.

29. McDermott, "William Clark's Struggle," 144; JLCE, 1:131n, 132n.

30. Jackson, *Stony Mountains,* 146.

31. John Francis McDermott, "The Library of John Hay of Cahokia and Belleville," *Bulletin of the Missouri Historical Society,* 1953, 9:183

32. Jackson, ed., *Letters,* 1:155n.

33. Lewis to Jefferson, 28 December 1803, Jackson, ed., *Letters,* 1:148-151.

34. Lewis to Jefferson, 28 December 1803, 1:150.

35. Lewis to Jefferson, 28 December 1803, 1:151.

36. Ambrose, *Undaunted Courage,* 123-124.

37. Lewis to Auguste Chouteau, 4 January 1804, Jackson, ed., *Letters,* 1:161.

38. Financial Records of the Expedition, 5 August 1807, Jackson, ed., *Letters,* 2:419-431; Ambrose, *Undaunted Courage,* 96-97, 130.

39. Lewis's receipt to Amos Stoddard, 1 December 1803, Jackson, ed., *Letters,* 1:142.

40. Lewis to Clark, 17 December 1803, Jackson, ed., *Letters,* 1:144.

41. Osgood, ed., *Notes,* 8.

42. JLCE, 2:509-529.

43. Osgood, ed., *Notes,* 8.

44. Osgood, ed., *Notes,* 192.

45. Osgood, ed., *Notes,* 9.

46. Osgood, ed., *Notes,* 8.

47. JLCE, 2:143.

12. Counting the Days

1. Osgood, ed., *Notes,* 15.

2. Osgood, ed., *Notes,* 11.

3. Lewis Detachment Orders, 20 February 1804, JLCE, 2:174-175.

4. Lewis Detachment Orders, 3 March 1804, JLCE, 2:178-2:179.

5. JLCE, 1:179.

6. Osgood, ed., *Notes,* 29.

7. JLCE, Atlas: 7; Osgood, ed., *Notes,* 16; Lewis to Jefferson, 18 May 1804, Jackson, ed., *Letters,* 1:192-194, 194n, 195n; Allen, *Passage,* 155-159.

8. Allen, *Passage,* 160-167.

9. Osgood, ed., *Notes,* 27.

10. Reynolds, *Pioneer History,* 186-88.

11. JLCE, 2:153-154n.

12. Osgood, ed., *Notes,* 27.

13. Osgood, ed., *Notes,* 30.

14. Jackson, *Stony Mountains,* 152-153; Appleman, *Lewis and Clark's Exploration,* 73.

15. Order of Amos Stoddard, 9 March 1804, receiving Louisiana from the Spanish Government from Carlos Dehault Delassus, to the French government, Missouri Historical Society, St. Louis. Meriwether Lewis and Charles Gratiot witnessed the document.

16. Ambrose, *Undaunted Courage,* 129.

17. "Charles Gratiot Was an Ardent Patriot and Eminent Citizen," clipping from an unidentified newspaper, n.d., Gratiot Papers, Genealogy, Missouri Historical Society, St. Louis.

18. "Charles Gratiot Was an Ardent Patriot and Eminent Citizen."

19. Osgood, ed., *Notes,* 27n.

20. Appleman, *Lewis and Clark's Exploration,* 67-68.

21. Osgood, ed., *Notes,* 29-30.

22. Lewis and Clark Detachment Order, 1 April 1804, JLCE, 190; JLCE, Appendix A, 2:510-512.

23. Clarke, *Men of the Lewis and Clark Expedition,* 23-24.

24. John Ordway to His Parents, 8 April 1804, Jackson, ed., *Letters,* 1:176-177.

25. Ronda, *Indians,* 14-15.

26. Jackson, ed., *Letters,* 1:171n, 172n.

27. Clark to Lewis, April 1804, Jackson, ed., *Letters,* 1:175.

28. JLCE, 2:225n-2:226n

29. Henry Dearborn to Lewis, 26 March 1804, Jackson, ed., *Letters,* 1:172, 172n.

30. Lewis to Clark, 3 May 1804, Jackson, ed., *Letters,* 1:179-180.

31. Ambrose, *Undaunted Courage,* 134-136.
32. All summaries of the field notes made by Clark in May are from Osgood, ed., *Notes,* 37, 38.
33. JLCE, 2:214-15.
34. Osgood, ed., *Notes,* 38.

13. Unlocking the Missouri

1. Jefferson to Lewis, 16 November 1803, Jackson, ed., *Letters,* 1:136-140.
2. Nasatir, ed., *Before Lewis and Clark,* 1:93-115.
3. John Francis McDermott, "Jean Baptiste Truteau and the Company of the Upper Missouri," undated and unpublished, McDermott Research Collection, Southern Illinois University-Edwardsville, 1-5; also Nasastir, "Truteau," *The Mountain Men and the Fur Trade of the Far West,* 1966, 81-94.
4. Nasatir, "Clamorgan," 86-94.
5. McDermott, "Truteau," 4.
6. Clamorgan's Instructions to Truteau, 30 June 1794, Nasatir, ed., *Before Lewis and Clark,* 1:243-253.
7. Nasatir, "Truteau," 388.
8. Nasatir, ed., *Before Lewis and Clark,* 1:91-93.
9. McDermott, "Truteau," 2; Nasatir, ed., *Before Lewis and Clark,* 1:91.
10. Ronda, *Indians,* 12.
11. Ronda, 11; Allen, *Passage,* 153-154.
12. JLCE, 2:154n; Nasatir, "James Mackay," *The Mountain Men and the Fur Trade of the Far West,* 1966, 185-187.
13. Nasatir, "McKay's Journal," ed., *Before Lewis and Clark,* 2:493.
14. JLCE, 2:6-7.
15. Aubrey Diller, "James Mackay's Journey in Nebraska in 1796," *Nebraska History,* 36:126.
16. Ronda, introduction to the 1990 edition of Nasatir, ed., *Before Lewis and Clark,* 2:vii.
17. Nasatir, ed., *Before Lewis and Clark,* 1:106-108.

18. Nasatir, "Mackay," 188; Gayoso de Lemos to Francisco Saavedra, New Orleans, 22 November 1798, Nasatir, ed., *Before Lewis and Clark*, 2: 582-586.

19. Nasatir, "Mackay," 205.

20. Osgood, ed., *Notes*, 16.

21. Jackson, ed., *Letters*, 155; Ronda, *Indians*, 10-11.

22. Studies of the Mackay and Evans maps include Allen, *Passage*, Jackson, "A New Lewis and Clark Map," *Bulletin of the Missouri Historical Society*, 1978; and the introduction by Moulton to the atlas, JLCE.

23. Lewis to Jefferson, 28 December 1803, Jackson, ed., *Letters*, 1:155.

24. Allen, *Passage*, 141n.

25. Allen, *Passage*, 142.

26. Ronda, *Indians*, 14.

27. JLCE, atlas: 6-7.

28. Jackson, ed., *Letters*, 1:135n.

29. Harrison to Clark, 13 November 1803, Jackson, ed., *Letters*, 1:135.

30. William Henry Harrison to Jefferson, 26 November 1803, Jackson, ed., *Letters*, 1:140-141.

31. Jefferson to Lewis, 13 January 1804, Jackson, ed., *Letters*, 1:163.

32. Garrison, "M. Austin's Journey," 533-534.

33. Nasatir, ed., *Before Lewis and Clark*, 1:115.

14. Three Cheers

1. JLCE, 9:1 (Ordway).

2. JLCE, 11:1 (Whitehouse).

3. Osgood, ed., *Notes*, 41.

4. Osgood, ed., *Notes*, 41.

5. JLCE, 2:233.

6. JLCE, 18 May 1804, 11:10 (Whitehouse).

7. Clark to William Croghan, 21 May 1804, Jackson, ed., *Letters*, 1:195-196.

8. Osgood, ed., *Notes*, 42.

9. Ambrose, *Undaunted Courage*, 137-138; JLCE, 1:243, 243n.

10. JLCE, 2:240.

11. JLCE, 2:241.

12. JLCE, 2:244.

13. JLCE, 9:6 (Ordway).

14. JLCE, 9:374 (Floyd).

15. JLCE, 10:8 (Gass).

16. JLCE, 11:11 (Whitehouse).

17. Amos Stoddard to Henry Dearborn, 3 June 1804, Jackson, ed., *Letters*, 1:196.

18. Biographical information on Dickson appears in Frank Dickson, "Hard on the Heels of Lewis and Clark," *Montana, the Magazine of Western History*, 1976, 14-25. Dickson was a great-great grandson of Joseph Dickson. Also, C.W. Butterfield, *History of Grant County, Wisconsin*, Madison, 1881, 553; and *Wisconsin Collections*, State Historical Society of Wisconsin, Personal Narratives for the years 1867, 1868, and 1869, by Col. Joseph Dickson, 315-317.

19. Dickson, "Hard on the Heels of Lewis and Clark," 16. Hancock is identified in a number of sources as an Illinoisan, including the journals of Lewis and Clark. However, the author could find no evidence he lived in Illinois country at any time.

20. JLCE, 8:158n.

21. Reuben G. Thwaites, editor, *Original Journals of the Lewis and Clark Expedition, 1804-1806* (New York: Dodd, Mead, 1904-05) 4:329.

22. JLCE, 9:348 (Ordway).

23. JLCE, 8:157.

24. Burton Harris, *John Colter: His Years in the Rockies* (New York: Scribner's, 1952), 35-36.

25. JLCE, 8:302.

26. After several years in the Belleville area, Dickson relocated to the Sangamon River in central Illinois where he again was among the first to explore frontier territory. W.P. Strickland, editor, *Autobiography of Peter Cartwright: The Backwoods Preacher* (Cranston & Stowe, 1856).

27. JLCE, 8:368-369; JLCE, 9:366 (Ordway). " . . . Here we found a widdow woman who we left here & has a plantation under tollarable good way Since we have been on the Expedition. . . ." This would have been the "widow Meacham," as identified by Thomas E. Lippincott.

28. JLCE, 8:370-8:371.

29. Lewis to Jefferson, 23 September 1806, Jackson, ed., *Letters*, 1:319-324.

30. Jefferson to Lewis, 26 October 1806, Jackson, ed., *Letters*, 1:350-351.

31. Ronda, "St. Louis Welcomes Lewis and Clark," *Voyages of Discovery: Essays on the Lewis and Clark Expedition* (Helena: Montana Historical Society Press, 1998), 203-205. Ronda says a party was held at a St. Louis inn, operated by William Christy, shortly after the Corps of Discovery arrived. The only report of the festivities and the toasts appeared in the Frankfort, Kentucky, *Western World,* for 11 October 1806. Ronda credits the Filson Club, Louisville, Kentucky, for providing a copy of the article.

32. Ambrose, *Undaunted Courage*, 414, 415-416; Donald Jackson, "William Clark and the Girls on the Pony," *Among the Sleeping Giants: Occasional Pieces on Lewis & Clark* (Urbana: University of Illinois Press, 1987), 33-42; also Steffen, *Clark*.

33. Ambrose provides a thorough discussion of Lewis's suicide, *Undaunted Courage*, 463-468.

34. Reynolds, *Pioneer History*, 302.

35. Jackson, ed., *Letters*, 2:638-639.

36. Skarsten, *George Drouillard*, 251-313.

37. Lewis to Henry Dearborn, 15 January 1807, Jackson, ed., *Letters,* 1:368-69.

SELECT BIBLIOGRAPHY

Collections, Manuscripts and Papers

American State Papers, Miscellaneous and Public Lands volumes.

Burton Collections, Detroit Public Library: John Askin Papers, John Edgar Papers, William Edgar Letters, Otto Fisher Papers, Jehu Hay Papers, Shelburne Manuscripts.

Chicago Historical Society: John Edgar documents.

Louisa H. Bowen Archives and Special Collections, Lovejoy Library, Southern Illinois University-Edwardsville: John Francis McDermott Collection; *Metro-East Journal* morgue.

Michigan Pioneer and Historical Society Collections, Detroit: Jehu Hay Papers.

Missouri Historical Society, Missouri History Museum, Library and Research Center, St. Louis: Gabriel Cerre Papers, Chouteau Collection, Auguste Chouteau Papers, Pierre Chouteau Papers, Charles Gratiot Papers, Fur Trade Papers, Louisiana Purchase Transfer Papers, Lucas Collection, Morrison Family Papers, St. Charles Papers, St. Louis Annals, Tiffany Family Papers.

Wisconsin State Historical Society: Lyman C. Draper Manuscripts: John Edgar, Rachel Edgar, Simon Kenton (microfilm).

Books

Allen, John Logan. *Passage Through the Garden: Lewis and Clark and the Image of the American Northwest.* Urbana: University of Illinois Press, 1975.

Allen, John W. *Legends and Lore of Southern Illinois*. Carbondale: Southern Illinois University Press, 1963.

Alvord, Clarence Walworth. *The Illinois Country, 1673-1818*. 1920. Reprint, Urbana: University of Illinois Press, 1987.

Ambrose, Stephen E. *Undaunted Courage: Meriwether Lewis, Thomas Jefferson and the Opening of the American West*. New York: Simon and Schuster, 1996.

Appleman, Roy. *Lewis and Clark's Transcontinental Exploration, 1804-1806*. 1975. Reprint, Washington, D.C.: National Park Service, 2000.

Bakeless, John. *Background to Glory: The Life of George Rogers Clark*. Philadelphia: Lippincott, 1957.

Baldwin, Carl R. *Echoes of Their Voices: A Saga of the Pioneers Who Pushed the Frontier to the Mississippi*. St. Louis: Hawthorne Publishing Co., 1978.

Bareis, Charles J., and James W. Porter, editors. *American Bottom Archaeology*. Urbana: University of Illinois Press, 1993.

Barnhart, John D. *Henry Hamilton and George Rogers Clark in the American Revolution with Unpublished Journal of Lieut. Gov. Henry Hamilton*. Crawfordsville, 1951.

Barnhart, John D., and Dorothy L. Riker. *Indiana to 1816: The Colonial Period*. Indianapolis: Indiana Historical Bureau & Indiana Historical Society, 1976.

Belting, Natalia M. *Kaskaskia Under the French Regime*. Urbana: University of Illinois Press, 1948.

Billington, Ray Allen. *Westward Expansion: A History of the America Frontier*. New York: Macmillan Company, 1949.

Boggess, Arthur Clinton. *The Settlement of Illinois: 1778-1830*. Chicago Historical Society, 1908.

Breese, Sidney. *The Early History of Illinois from Its Discovery by the French, 1673*. Chicago: E.B. Myers, 1884.

Brink, W.R. & Co., publisher. *The History of Madison County, Illinois 1682-1882*. Edwardsville, 1882.

Buck, Solon J. *Illinois in 1818*. Urbana: University of Illinois Press, 1967.

Burton, Clarence M., editor. *The City of Detroit, Michigan, 1701-1922.* Detroit: S.J.Clarke Publishing Company, 1922.

Campbell, Marjorie Wilkins. *The North West Company.* New York: St. Martin's Press, 1957.

Carter, Clarence Edwin, compiler and editor. *The Territorial Papers of the United States: The Territory of Indiana, 1801-1809.* Washington: Government Printing Office, 1939.

_____. *The Territorial Papers of the United States: The Territory Northwest of the River Ohio, 1787-1803.* Washington: Government Printing Office,1934, volumes II and III.

Cartwright, Peter. *Autobiography of Peter Cartwright: The Backwoods Preacher.* W. P. Strickland, editor. Cincinnati: Cranston & Stowe, 1856.

Clark, William. *The Field Notes of Captain William Clark, 1803-05.* Ernest Staples Osgood, editor. New Haven: Yale University, 1964.

Clarke, Charles G. *The Men of the Lewis and Clark Expedition.* Glendale: Arthur H. Clark, 1970.

Chittenden, Hiram Martin. *A History of the American Fur Trade of the Far West.* Stanford: Academic Reprints, 1954. Two volumes.

Cleaves, Freeman. *Old Tippecanoe: William Henry Harrison and His Time.* New York: Scribner's, 1939.

Coues, Elliott, editor. *History of the Expedition Under the Command of Lewis and Clark.* New York: Dover Publications, 1965. Three volumes.

Cutright, Paul Russell. *A History of the Lewis and Clark Journals.* Norman: University of Oklahoma Press, 1976.

Davis, James E. *Frontier Illinois.* Bloomington: Indiana University Press, 1998.

Dillon, Richard. *Meriwether Lewis.* New York: Coward, McCann, 1965.

Eckberg, Carl J. *French Roots in the Illinois Country: The Mississippi Frontier in Colonial Times.* Urbana: University of Illinois Press, 1998.

Eckert, Allan W. *The Frontiersmen: A Narrative.* Boston: Little, Brown, 1967.

Farmer, Silas. *History of Detroit and Wayne County and Early Michigan.*

Detroit: Silas Farmer and Co., 1890.

Foley, William E., and C. David Rice. *The First Chouteaus: River Barons of Early St. Louis.* Urbana: University of Illinois Press, 1983.

Goebel, Dorothy B. *William Henry Harrison: A Political Biography.* Philadelphia: Porcupine Press, 1974.

Harris, Burton. *John Colter: His Years in the Rockies.* New York: Scribner's, 1952.

Howard, Robert P. *Illinois: A History of the Prairie State.* Grand Rapids: Eerdmans Publishing Co., 1972.

Jackson, Donald, editor. *Letters of the Lewis and Clark Expedition with Related Documents, 1783-1854.* Urbana: University of Illinois Press, 1978. Two volumes.

_____. *Thomas Jefferson & the Stony Mountains: Exploring the West from Monticello.* Urbana: University of Illinois Press, 1981.

James, James Alton, editor. *George Rogers Clark Papers, 1771-1781.* Collections of the Illinois State Historical Library, Springfield, 1912, volume three.

Kenton, Edna. *Simon Kenton: His Life and Period, 1755-1836.* New York: Doubleday, 1930.

Lewis, Meriwether, and William Clark. *The Journals of the Lewis and Clark Expedition.* Gary E. Moulton, editor. Lincoln: University of Nebraska Press, 1983-2001. Thirteen volumes.

McDermott, John Francis, editor. *Old Cahokia: A Narrative and Documents Illustrating the First Century of Its History.* St. Louis: Historical Documents Foundation, 1949.

_____. *Frenchmen and French Ways in the Mississippi Valley.* Urbana: University of Illinois Press, 1969.

_____. *The French in the Mississippi Valley.* Urbana: University of Illinois Press, 1965.

McDonough, J. L., publisher. *History of Randolph, Monroe and Perry Counties, Illinois.* Philadelphia, 1883.

Morton, W. L. *Manitoba: A History.* Toronto: University of Toronto Press, 1967.

Nasatir, Abraham, editor. *Before Lewis and Clark: Documents Illustrat-*

ing the History of The Missouri, 1785-1804. 1952. Reprint, Lincoln: University of Nebraska Press, 1990. Two volumes.

_____. *Borderland in Retreat: From Spanish Louisiana to the Far Southwest.* Albuquerque: University of New Mexico Press, 1976.

Olgesby, Richard Edward. *Manuel Lisa and the Opening of the Missouri Fur Trade.* Norman: University of Oklahoma Press, 1963.

Pease, Theodore Calvin and Marguerite Jenison Pease. George *Rogers Clark and the Revolution in Illinois, 1763-1787.* Springfield: Illinois State Historical Library, 1929.

Philbrick, Francis S., editor, *Collections of the Illinois State Historical Library: The Laws of Indiana Territory, 1801-1809.* Springfield: Illinois State Historical Library, 1930.

Phillips, Paul Chrisler. *The Fur Trade.* Norman: University of Oklahoma Press, 1961. Two volumes.

Quaife, Milo M., editor. *The Journals of Captain Meriwether Lewis and Sergeant John Ordway, Kept on the Expedition of Western Exploration, 1803-1806.* Madison: The State Historical Society of Wisconsin, 1916.

_____. *The Capture of Old Vincennes.* Indianapolis: Indiana Historical Society, 1927.

Reynolds, John. *The Pioneer History of Illinois.* Belleville: N.A. Randall, 1852.

Rokker, H. W., publisher. *A Complete History of Illinois from 1673 to 1884.* Springfield, 1884.

Ronda, James P. *Lewis and Clark among the Indians.* Lincoln: University of Nebraska Press, 1984.

Seineke, Kathrine Wagner, editor. *Pierre Menard Collection.* Springfield: Illinois State Historical Society, 1972.

_____. *The George Rogers Clark Adventure in the Illinois.* New Orleans: Polyanthos, 1981.

Skarsten, M.O. *George Drouillard, Hunter and Interpreter for Lewis and Clark, and Fur Trader, 1807-1810.* Glendale: Arthur H. Clark, 1964.

Sosin, Jack M. *The Revolutionary Frontier, 1763-1783.* New York: Holt, Rinehart and Winston, 1967.

Steffen, Jerome O. *William Clark: Jeffersonian Man on the Frontier.* Norman: University of Oklahoma, 1977.

Stoddard, Major Amos. *Sketches, Historical and Descriptive of Louisiana.* Philadelphia: Mathew Carey, 1812.

Thornbrough, Gayle, editor. *Outpost on the Wabash, 1787-1791.* Indianapolis: Indiana Historical Society, 1957.

Thwaites, Reuben Gold. *The Original Journals of the Lewis and Clark Expedition.* New York: Dodd, Mead, 1904-05. Eight volumes.

Wilderman, A. S., and A. A. Wilderman, editors. *Historical Encyclopedia of Illinois and History of St. Clair County.* Chicago: Munsell Publishing, 1907.

Articles, Documents, Dissertations, Newspapers

Able-Henderson, Annie H. "Mackay's Table of Distances." *Missouri Valley Historical Review,* 10:428-46.

Allen, John Logan. "Geographical Knowledge and American Images of the Louisiana Territory." *Voyages of Discovery: Essays on the Lewis and Clark Expedition.* Missoula: Montana Historical Society Press, 1998.

Allinson, May. "The Government of Illinois, 1790-1799." *Illinois State Historical Society Proceedings,* 12 (1907) 277-292.

Babb, Margaret E. "The Mansion House of Cahokia and Its Builder— Nicholas Jarrot." *Transactions of the Illinois State Historical Society,* 1924, 78-93.

Billington, Ray Allen. "The Frontier in Illinois History." *Journal of the Illinois State Historical Society,* Spring, 1950, 28-45.

Birk, Douglas A. "John Sayer and the Fond du Lac Trade: The North West Company in Minnesota and Wisconsin," *Rendezvous: Selected Papers of the Fourth North American Fur Trade Conference, 1981.* St. Paul, 51-62.

Bloom, Jo Tice. "The Territorial Delegates of Indiana Territory, 1801-1816." *The Old Northwest.* Fall, 1980, 7-22.

Boylan, Rose Jo. *East St. Louis Journal.* Various articles, Lovejoy Library, Southern Illinois University-Edwardsville, 1950-62.

Burt, W. A., editor. "John Rice Jones: A Brief Sketch of the Life and Public Career of the First Practicing Lawyer of Illinois." *Chicago Historical Society's Collections,* 4: 230-40.

Caldwell, Norman W. "Fort Massac During the French and Indian War." *Journal of the Illinois State Historical Society,* 1950, 100-119.

_____. "Fort Massac: The American Frontier Post, 1778-1806." *Journal of the Illinois State Historical Society,* 1950, 265-281.

_____ . "Fort Massac: Since 1805." *Journal of the Illinois Historical Society,* 1951, 47-60.

Clanton, Helen. "Restoring 150-Year-Old Cahokia Home." *St. Louis Post-Dispatch,* 18 April 1948.

Dickson, Col. Joseph. "Personal Narratives." *Collections of the State Historical Society of Wisconsin, Madison, 1868,* 815-17.

Dickson, Frank H. "Joseph Dickson." *The Mountain Men and the Fur Trade of the Far West.* Glendale: Arthur H. Clark, 1966, 71-79.

_____."Hard on the Heels of Lewis and Clark." *Montana, the Magazine of Western History,* January (1976) 14-25.

Diller, Aubrey. "James Mackay's Journey in Nebraska in 1796." *Nebraska History,* 36 (1955), 123-128.

Fietsam, Robert C. Jr. "The Lewis and Clark Expedition Winter Base of Operations at Camp DuBois." *Journal of the St. Clair County Historical Society,* 1996, 11-33.

Fortier, John B. "New Light on Fort Massac." *Frenchmen and French Ways in the Mississippi Valley.* Urbana: University of Illinois Press, 1969.

Garrison, George P., editor. "A Memorandum of M. Austin's Journey. . . ." *American Historical Review,* 5 (1900) 518-42.

Gieseker, Brenda R. "A Business Venture at Cahokia: The Letters of Charles Gratiot, 1778-1779." *Old Cahokia: A Narrative and Documents Illustrating the First Century of Its History.* St. Louis: Historical Documents Foundation, 1949, 190-231.

Hanley, Sarah Bond. "In the Early Days." *Journal of the Illinois State Historical Society,* 22 (1930) 659-63.

Jackson, Donald. "Some Books Carried by Lewis and Clark." *Bulletin of the Missouri Historical Society,* 1959, 3-13.

_____."A New Lewis and Clark Map." *Bulletin of the Missouri Historical Society,* January, 1961.

Jenks, William L. "Diary of the Siege of Detroit." *Michigan History Magazine,* 12 (1928), 437-442.

Lankiewicz, Donald P. "The Camp on Wood River: A Winter of Preparation for the Lewis and Clark Expedition." *Journal of the Illinois State Historical Society,* 1982, 115-120.

Large, Arlen. "Additions to the Party: How an Expedition Grew and Grew." *We Proceeded On,* 16 (1990).

Lippincott, Rev. Thomas E. "Early Days in Madison County." Manuscript papers, rare book collection, Southern Illinois University-Edwardsville, Lovejoy Library.

Loos, John Louis. "A Biography of William Clark, 1770-1813." Doctoral dissertation, Washington University, 1953.

_____. "William Clark's Part in the Preparation of the Lewis and Clark Expedition." *Bulletin of the Missouri Historical Society,* 1954, 490-511.

McDermott, John Francis. "The Library of John Hay of Cahokia and Belleville." *Bulletin of the Missouri Historical Society,* 9 (1953)183-186.

_____. "Captain Stoddard Discovers St. Louis." *Bulletin of the Missouri Historical Society,* 10 (1954), 328-335.

_____. "The Western Journals of Dr. George Hunter." *Transactions of the American Philosophical Society,* 53, July, 1963.

_____."William Clark's Struggle With Place Names in Upper Louisiana." *Bulletin of the Missouri Historical Society.* (1978) 34:140-50.

_____. "Jean Baptiste Truteau and the Company of the Upper Missouri." Undated and unpublished, McDermott research collection, Southern Illinois University-Edwardsville, Lovejoy Library.

McGrane, Reginald E., editor. "William Clark's Journal of General Wayne's Campaign." *Mississippi Valley Historical Review,* 1:418-444.

Mohrman, Mary S. "Jarrot House: Her First 150 Years." *Journal of the St. Clair County Historical Society,* 1 (1966) 21-23.

Morton, W. L. "The North West Company: Pedlars Extraordinary."

Aspects of the Fur Trade, Minnesota Historical Society, 1967, 9-17.

Nasatir, Abraham. "Anglo-Spanish Rivalry in the Iowa Country, 1797-1798." *The Iowa Journal of History and Politics,* 28 (1930) 337-389.

_____. "The Anglo-Spanish Frontier on the Upper Mississippi, 1786-1796." *The Iowa Journal of History and Politics,* 29 (1931) 55-200.

_____. "James Mackay." *The Mountain Men and the Fur Trade in the Far West,* Glendale: Arthur H. Clark, 1966, 185-206.

_____."Jacques Clamorgan." *The Mountain Men and the Fur Trade of the Far West,* Glendale: Arthur H. Clark, 1966, 81-94.

_____ . "Jean Baptiste Truteau." *The Mountain Men of the Fur Trade in the Far West,* Glendale: Arthur H. Clark, 1966, 381-397.

Olgesby, Richard Edward. "William Morrison." *The Mountain Men and the Fur Trade of the Far West,* Glendale: Arthur Clark, 1966, 197-203.

Peterson, Charles E. "Notes on Old Cahokia." Parts I, II, III, *Journal of the Illinois State Historical Society,* 42 (1948), 7-29, 193-208, 313-43.

Quaife, Milo M., editor. "A Narrative of Life on the Old Frontier: Henry Hay's Journal from Detroit to the Mississippi River." *Indiana Historical Society Publications,* 7, 1921.

_____. "Extracts from Capt. McKay's Journal—and Others." *Wisconsin Historical Society Proceedings,* 1916, 186-209.

_____. "Detroit Biographies: Jehu Hay." *Burton Historical Collection Leaflet,* 1929, 1-16.

Roberts, James H. "The Life and Times of General John Edgar." *Transactions of the Illinois State Historical Society,* 12 (1907) 64-73.

Ronda, James P. "'A Most Perfect Harmony': The Lewis and Clark Expedition as an Exploration Community." *Voyages of Discovery: Essays on the Lewis and Clark Expedition,* Missoula: Montana Historical Society Press, 1998.

Saucier, Walter J., and Kathrine Wagner Seineke. "Francois Saucier, Engineer of Fort de Chartres, Illinois." *Frenchmen and French Ways in the Mississippi Valley,* Urbana: University of Illinois Press, 1969.

Sparks, Everett, L. "Where the Trail Begins: The Illinois Legacy to the

Lewis and Clark Expedition." *We Proceeded On*, February, 1988, 4-9.

Tevebaugh, John L. "Merchant on the Western Frontier: William Morrison of Kaskaskia, 1790-1837." Doctoral dissertation, University of Illinois, 1962.

Thomas, Samuel W. "William Clark's 1795 and 1797 Journals and Their Significance." *Bulletin of the Missouri Historical Society*, (1969) 25: 279-295.

Thorne, Tanis Chapman. "The Chouteau Family and the Osage Trade: A Generational Study." *Rendezvous: Selected Papers of the Fourth North American Fur Trade Conference, 1981,* 109-120.

Whiteside, Don. "Family Manuscript." Revisions by William R. Whiteside, January, 2000, Cottage Hills, Illinois.

Woolard, F. M. "Route of Colonel George Rogers Clark and His Army From Kaskaskia to Vincennes." *Journal of the Illinois State Historical Society,* 12: 48-63.

INDEX

Edwards Brothers,Inc!
Thorofare, NJ 08086
22 March, 2011
BA2011081